CAREER TREK

CAREER TREK

YOUR PROFESSIONAL BUDDY

CLIMB
WITH CLARITY.
LEAD WITH
IMPACT.

COACH RAM

JAICO PUBLISHING HOUSE

Ahmedabad Bangalore Chennai
Delhi Hyderabad Kolkata Mumbai

Published by Jaico Publishing House
A-2 Jash Chambers, 7-A Sir Phirozshah Mehta Road
Fort, Mumbai - 400 001
jaicopub@jaicobooks.com
www.jaicobooks.com

CAREER TREK
ISBN 978-93-49358-87-4

First Jaico Impression: 2025

Page design and layout by Jojy Philip, Delhi

Inside Illustrations: Sabina Vinod

Printed by
Thomson Press India Limited, New Delhi

CONTENTS

01	**What Is Your Career Wheel?** What makes your career unique?	1
02	**Find Your Career Compass** Learn the patterns of your career trajectory	9
03	**What Are Your Career Anchors?** Find out what motivates you to choose your career	23
04	**Do You Have Your PBOD?** Set up your personal board of directors to guide your career out of the rut	37
05	**Derailers and Drivers for Growth** Factors that can make or break your career	53
06	**Managing Professional Relationships** Build win-win relationships at work	67
07	**Showcasing Impact** Master the art of marketing yourself	85

08 **Dealing with Dilemmas** 99

Gain clarity into your values and vision

09 **Manufacturing Your Luck** 111

Discover the secret of making your own luck

10 **Individual Development Plans (IDPs)** 125

The roadmap to chart your career destiny

11 **Building a Personal Brand** 141

The 101 of your personal brand

12 **Managing Career Transitions** 151

Beat your mid-career blues

13 **Future-Proofing Your Career** 165

Build a career for long-term success

14 **Hard Truths of Corporations** 179

The shocking reality of the corporate world

15 **Rapid Fire Round with Coach Ram** 187

Coach Ram's quick-fire tips and insights on your career

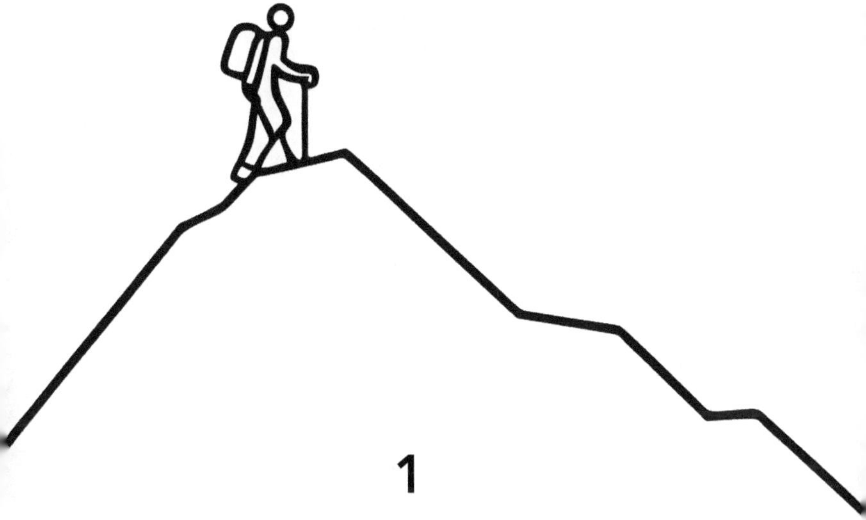

1

What Is Your Career Wheel?

What makes your career unique?

Careers are a fascinating, complex, and deeply personal journey. Crafting one's career is influenced by many factors. I see the career journey as a trek rather than a marathon or a sprint.

Imagine a vast mountain range. Each peak is unique in its height, view, and terrain. These peaks symbolize the various definitions of career success. For some, success is about the job title; for others, it's freedom, their impact, financial prosperity, personal fulfillment, or a combination of these elements.

I have coached numerous professionals in making career decisions since 2012. Most of my clientele is 30-45 years of age with close to a decade of work experience. I've found that many individuals are clear about what type of work they dislike but struggle to identify what inspires them. While the concept of Ikigai—the intersection of passion, skill, market demand, and financial viability—has guided many on their quest to find a job that's the right fit for them, it only addresses the "what and why" of careers, leaving the "how" and other influencing factors largely unexplored.

In my experience, familiar sayings like, "Do what you love, and you'll never work a day in your life," underscore a limited understanding of how individuals perceive their careers. To understand the factors of professional success, I conducted a study involving over 600 diverse professionals in October 2023 where participants across different organizations and age groups were well represented. Through their responses to the online survey they shared insights on their careers. The goal of the career study was to unravel the mystery of accomplishment and the values that guide individuals in their career choices. The result? The "Career Wheel."

Take Raj, for instance—a 25-year-old hailing from a tier-3 town and is now building his career in Bangalore. His Ikigai revolves around the art of driving—a clear "what." He excels at it, there's a market for his skills, and he derives genuine pleasure from it. Yet, there remain various "how's" to explore—becoming an Ola or Uber driver, serving as a dedicated chauffeur, joining a company with a fleet of vehicles, or even becoming a solopreneur. Each choice comes with a distinct lifestyle, complete with its own advantages and disadvantages.

Even after uncovering one's Ikigai, professionals make career choices influenced by a range of other factors.

Insights from the 600 plus people I surveyed reveal the reasons why career professionals choose their next career role. Interestingly, the significance of factors like Brand & Title and Pay diminished for those above 60 years of age, while Growth Potential and a Positive Workplace Culture gained importance. However, the reasons why professionals chose their present roles also fluctuated with different age groups. In conclusion, individual preferences—often unspoken and unquestioned—are the ultimate compass in career related decision-making.

Shruti, a design professional in Chennai, one of the individuals I coached, offers a profound illustration of the deeply rooted significance of title, designation, and brand. Her eagerness to secure validation from her parents underpinned her prioritization of the above variables. She preferred offers from popular brands that gave societal validation even if other offers with lesser-known brands came with a better role. Knowing that this belief was driving her decision-making, Shruti rewired her mind to look at her career holistically. She stopped making decisions that pleased her parents. She looked at making career decisions based on what will give her exposure, allow her to learn and grow even if the organization or brand was less popular. She felt liberated as she owned her career choices and felt more authentic.

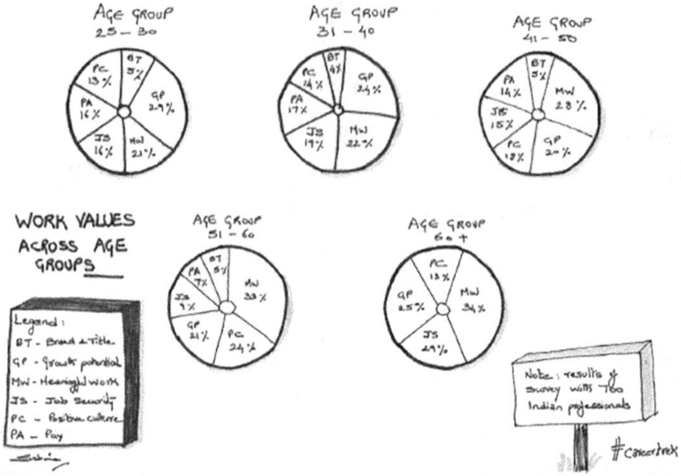

As you can see, the importance of Brand & Title declines with age, while the desire for Meaningful Work increases, particularly among those aged 60 and above. This shift emphasizes how our work values mature over time.

Let's look at Gopal, a project manager working for a for-profit organization in social sector. I coached him in 2018 and have closely witnessed his career journey since then. His story will help you further understand the intricate nature of career choices. Despite prioritizing income or standard of living, Gopal lived modestly. In a conversation with him, I learned about the impact a financial crisis in his father's life had on him. His father moved from a job to being an entrepreneur. The business did not go well. They faced financial hardships and his father returned to a job with lot of debt to pay off. This experience shaped Gopal's perception of saving money. His childhood memory continues to influence Gopal's decisions even today, often subconsciously.

Bringing it all together, we find a rich diversity of career wheels among different age groups. The choices are as diverse as the individuals. As a coach, I've come to appreciate that every journey, every choice, and every influencing factor is unique to each person. The crux lies in cultivating self-awareness regarding our values, factors, and attitudes that influence our decisions—some of which may confine us, while others liberate us.

Another finding from my study is that, only 10% of professionals have sought the guidance of a professional coach. The International Coaching Federation's (IFC) research shows that career coaching helps individuals identify strengths, weaknesses, and career aspirations, leading to greater self-awareness, clarity, and growth. This presents a remarkable opportunity for you to partner with a coach, explore your career wheel and embark on a career trek that not only makes you more self-aware but also intentional and fulfilled. I want you to reflect on your career wheel. Fill your responses in the following chart to figure your career wheel.

MY CAREER WHEEL
Careertrek
Meaningful work
BPO
Brand & title
Job Security
growth potential
Positive Culture
Pay

NOTES :

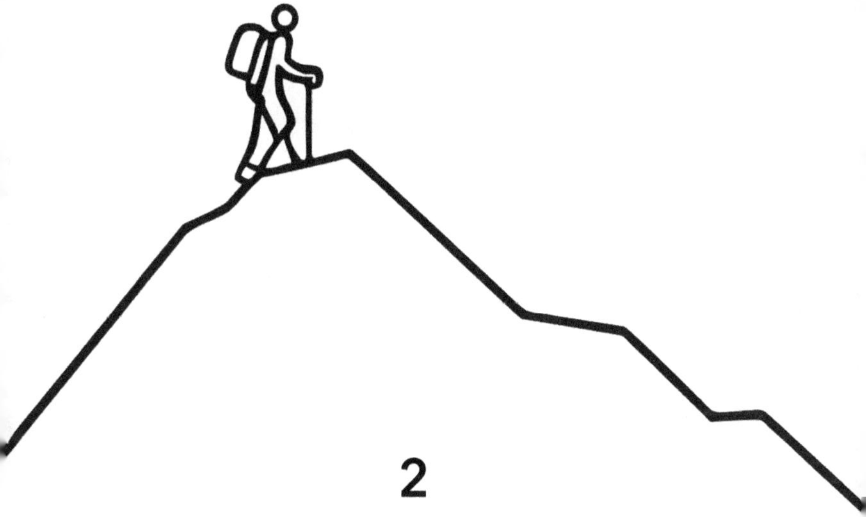

2

Find Your Career Compass

Learn the patterns of your career trajectory

In a world where careers are no longer linear but dynamic and multifaceted, 65% of professionals experience multiple career transitions. These statistics underscore a fundamental shift in how individuals perceive and navigate their professional paths.

The traditional view of a career as a linear climb up the corporate ladder is evolving. Professionals now have the autonomy to craft unique trajectories—be it through deep expertise, lateral growth, or embracing temporary transitions.

Comparisons are tempting. We indulge in it or witness people comparing our accomplishments with our peers or neighbors. Please know that two individuals cannot have the same career trajectory, and therefore, the comparison will never be fair. So, spare yourself the trouble. The decisions we make in our professional lives are as diverse as the trajectories we follow. Let's begin our exploration!

As the famous saying goes, "Life is the sum of all your choices." This resonates profoundly with our careers; each decision shapes the narrative of our professional story. Perhaps, that's why sometimes backbenchers make the most successful entrepreneurs! Their backbench experiences gave them enough space to reflect on themselves and gain clarity about their career trek.

I want you to reflect on the motivations driving your career decisions—whether they stem from a quest for power, a pursuit of mastery, a craving for creativity, or a desire for variety and independence.

Before we embark on this journey of self-discovery, allow me to invite you to an inner dialogue with yourself. Are you ready to pause, ponder, and navigate the depths of your career narrative?

Self-Reflective Questionnaire

1. Do you know the four types of career trajectories?
2. Do you know what linear, expert, spiral, and transitory career paths look like?
3. Do you know your preferred career path and how to find out the same?

To make your reading relatable and reflective, I want to share my learnings with you through, conversation. Here is Piyush, a young professional in his 30s, who found himself at a crossroads in his career. The possibilities before him, each path diverging into an unknown future, were many. Feeling overwhelmed and lost, he decided to seek my mentorship. I don't claim to know all the answers. In this book, my conversations with Piyush are a summary of all the sessions I have had with coachees over the years. I hope these insights help you.

One day, Piyush, who had attended one of my career webinars, texted me saying: "Coach, I've been doing some soul-searching about my career, and I feel like I'm standing at a fork in the road. I'm not sure which direction to take or what trajectory would be best for me. It's all a bit daunting."

I assured him that he was not alone in feeling that way. "Career decisions can be challenging, especially when you're faced with so many options. But fear not, my friend. Let's break it down together."

Piyush: That would be great, Coach. I've been reading about different career trajectories and it seems like there are so many paths one can take. How do I even begin to figure out which one is right for me?

Coach Ram: Well, you're already on the right track by exploring different options. Understanding the various career trajectories can give you valuable insights into the kinds of paths available to you. Have you heard about the four major types of career trajectories?

Piyush: Yes, I have. I came across them while researching career development. There's the linear trajectory, expert trajectory, spiral trajectory, and transitory trajectory, right?

Coach Ram: Exactly! Each trajectory offers a unique approach to career growth and development. Let's take a closer look at each one, shall we?

Piyush: Sure thing, Coach. So, the linear trajectory is all about climbing the ladder? It's like moving up step by step in a structured way.

Coach Ram: Absolutely, Piyush. The linear trajectory is like an ascent. Individuals who follow this path typically progress through ascending roles and increasing responsibilities within the same company or industry. It's the conventional climb up the corporate ladder where you are driven by motives like power and achievement.

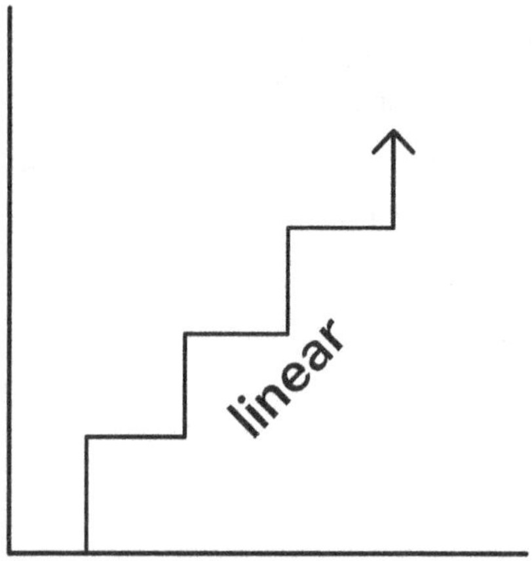

Piyush: Can you give me an example of what that looks like?

Coach Ram: Let's discuss Rajesh who started his career as a junior software engineer at a major IT company in Bangalore. He was very focused on his career from the beginning. He put in long hours, took on extra projects, and constantly sought ways to improve his skills.

After a few years, Rajesh was promoted to senior software engineer because of his hard work and dedication. He didn't stop there. Rajesh continued to excel and soon moved up to a team leader role where he was responsible for overseeing a group of engineers. His ability to lead and deliver projects on time and within budget caught the attention of higher management.

Eventually, Rajesh became a project manager, handling larger and more complex projects. His trajectory didn't stop there; he was later promoted to senior project manager, and now, he's aiming for a director role. Throughout his career, Rajesh has been driven by his desire to climb the corporate ladder, take on more responsibility and achieve greater success.

This is a classic example of a linear trajectory.

Piyush: Got it. It seems like a straightforward path but I imagine there must be challenges along the way.

Coach Ram: Absolutely, Piyush. While the linear trajectory offers a clear path to advancement, it's not without its challenges. Competition for higher positions can be fierce and individuals may face obstacles such as office politics, limited opportunities for growth, or the risk of stagnation. It's essential to stay focused and adaptable and also seek opportunities for growth.

Piyush: That's good to keep in mind. Now, let's talk about the expert trajectory. How does that differ from the linear path?

Coach Ram: The expert trajectory emphasizes depth over width (general management). Instead of continuous upward movement, individuals on this path focus on mastering a specific discipline. The driving forces here are mastery, expertise, and the assuredness of being an authority in a particular field.

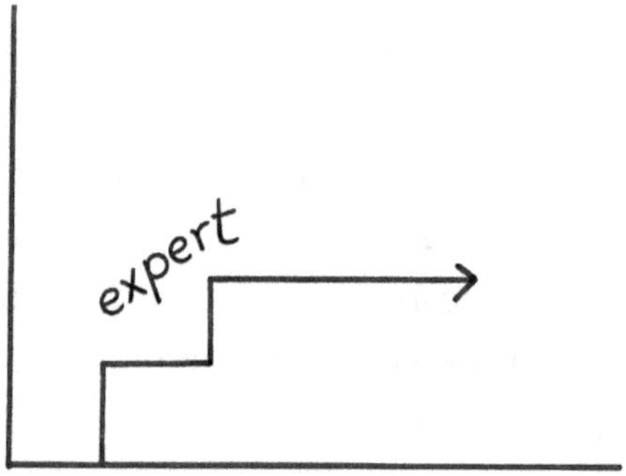

Piyush: So, rather than climbing the ladder, someone on the expert trajectory is focused on becoming a subject matter expert?

Coach Ram: Exactly! The expert trajectory involves immersing ourselves in a particular discipline, honing skills and gaining in-depth knowledge. It's about becoming a recognized expert in your field, through advanced education, certifications, or years of experience. The competencies include quality of input, commitment to deadlines, and technical skills.

Piyush: That sounds fascinating. It's like becoming a true master in your craft rather than just moving up the ranks.

Coach Ram: Precisely. The expert trajectory offers a different kind of fulfillment, driven by a passion for continuous learning and mastery. It's about depth rather than breadth. On this path, individuals find fulfillment in becoming sought-after experts with the required technical skills.

Piyush: I can see how rewarding that is. What about the spiral trajectory? How does that fit into the picture?

Coach Ram: The spiral trajectory involves lateral growth. Instead of moving strictly upward or focusing solely on depth, individuals on this path thrive in environments with cross-functional teams such as marketing, sales, human resources, etc., and diverse experiences. It's an exploration beyond the confines of a single discipline driven by personal growth and creativity.

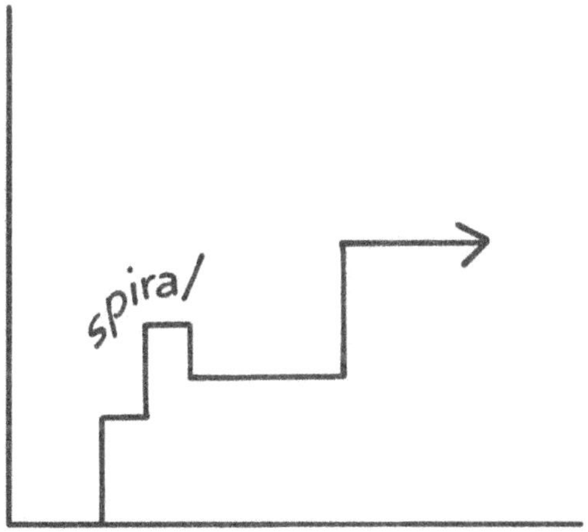

Piyush: That's appealing. What about the transitory trajectory? How does that differ from the others?

Coach Ram: The transitory trajectory comprises variety and independence. It involves shorter tenures. Rather than focusing on climbing the ladder or mastering a specific discipline, individuals on this path thrive on change and exploration (typically in consulting roles).

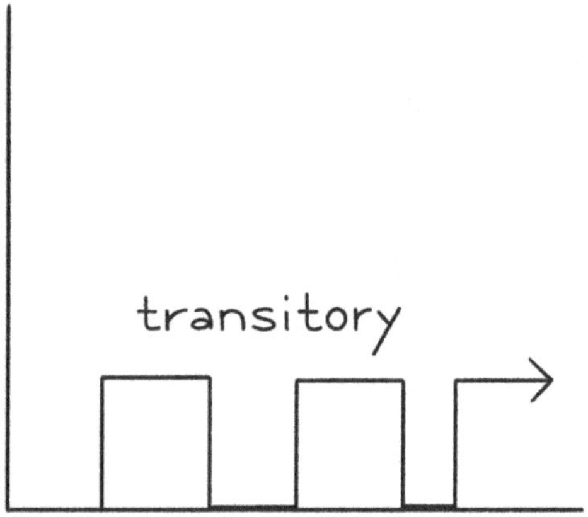

Piyush: So, it's about trying different things.

Coach Ram: Exactly. The transitory trajectory offers a career path that allows individuals to navigate different projects and roles. It's about flexibility, adaptability, and an openness to new opportunities. This trajectory is not limited to one domain or function. Instead, it focuses on building multiple career streams in line with your passion and values. For example, being a solopreneur or having a portfolio career.

Piyush: That's fascinating. It seems like each trajectory offers its unique path to career growth and fulfillment.

Coach Ram: The key is to understand your values, aspirations, and the journey that aligns with your vision of a fulfilling career. Whether you resonate with the linear climb, the expert's depth, the spiral's lateral dance, or the transitory exploration, each trajectory has its merits. Your choice depends on what drives you and where you see yourself thriving.

Take Dhriti, for example. Dhriti is a content writer who started her career as a freelancer while she was in college. After a few years, she wanted to challenge herself. So, she decided to move to a startup where she could explore different forms of writing, like blogging, SEO-based web content writing, creative writing, script writing, etc.

At the startup, Dhriti also worked on social media campaigns, content creation, digital marketing, AI integration, prompt engineering, and graphic design. Having gained diverse experiences there, she moved on to a non-profit organization where she managed its social media campaigns. Thus, she combined her skills with a cause that she was passionate about.

Years later, Dhriti explored performance arts as she always wanted to see her writings come to life. She performed on weekends. With time, she received job offers to host, perform, and conduct workshops. At these workshops, she helped various attendees with their writing and performing skills. This allowed her to work on short-term projects with individuals who had different skills and backgrounds.

Currently, Dhriti works as a public speaking coach. Suffice it to say, she enjoys the flexibility, the variety of skills, and challenges that every job offers. Exploration drives her career choices, and so she embraces a transitory career trajectory instead of a traditional career climb.

Piyush: Thank you, Coach. This has been incredibly insightful. I have a better understanding now of the different career trajectories and how they relate to my own career journey.

Coach Ram: You're welcome. Remember, your career journey is entirely personal. These trajectories serve as signposts that offer insights into the possible directions you can take. Take your time to reflect and explore. You'll find the path that's right for you.

Armed with newfound insights into the various career trajectories, Piyush embarked on his journey of self-discovery. He was ready to explore the possibilities that lay ahead.

What is your preferred career trajectory? Why?

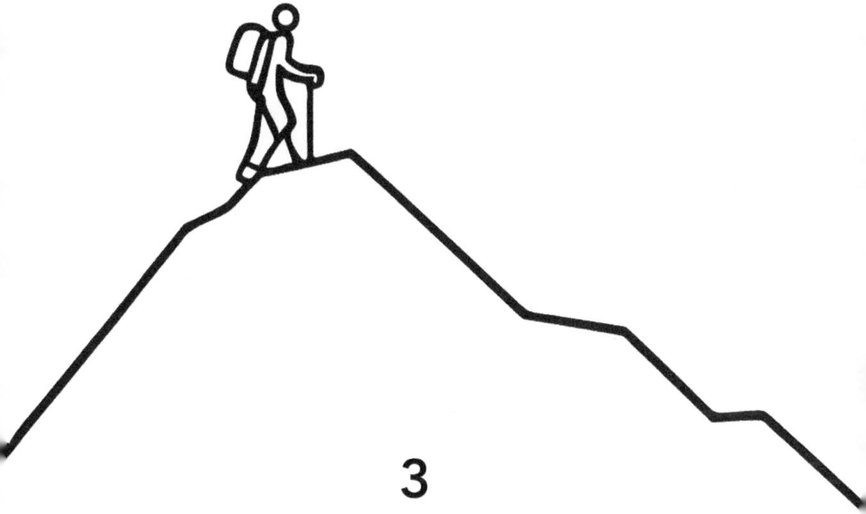

3

What Are Your Career Anchors?

Find out what motivates you to choose your career

After his conversation with Coach Ram, Piyush had some more questions. He sought the coach's guidance again.

Coach Ram: Piyush, what a pleasant surprise! I didn't expect you to run out of wisdom anytime soon or have I made you sleepless?

Piyush: I haven't been able to sleep. But it is not you, rather a question that's keeping me awake. I relate to all four trajectories. How do I know what's best for me?

Coach Ram: To find the right career path, you need career anchors.

Piyush: What are these?

Coach Ram: Career anchors guide our career choices and shape our professional identities. They are our core values, motivations, and competencies. They provide stability and direction to our career path.

Piyush: How do we determine what our career anchors are?

Coach Ram: There are various tools. Edgar Schein's framework outlines eight different types of career anchors. They range from technical competence to entrepreneurial creativity.

Piyush: Can you walk me through some of these career anchors?

Coach Ram: Let's delve into each career anchor one by one. First, let's talk about technical or functional competence. Individuals anchored in this competence are knowledgeable and motivated to excel in a particular field of specialization. They thrive on challenging technical work and prefer roles that allow them to leverage their expertise.

Piyush: That sounds like someone passionate about their field. How does this anchor affect their career choices?

Coach Ram: Let me tell you about Priya, a software engineer with a strong technical or functional competence anchor. Priya had a knack for coding and problem-solving since college. She excels in writing efficient algorithms and diving into complex technical challenges. Priya always chose roles that allowed her to work on cutting-edge technologies and software development projects. She's happiest when she codes and pushes the boundaries in her field.

Piyush: What about other career anchors?

Coach Ram: The next anchor is managerial competence. Individuals are driven by a desire to climb the corporate ladder and undertake more responsibilities. They excel in analytical, interpersonal, and emotional skills.

For example, think of a leader with a managerial competence anchor who has always been adept at organizing people and resources to achieve common goals. In his previous roles, he demonstrated strong leadership skills that earned him promotions to

managerial positions. He enjoys mentoring his team members. His career trajectory has been marked by a series of promotions. Every time, he gets closer to his goal of becoming a senior executive in his organization.

Piyush: That makes sense. What about the autonomy or independence anchor?

Coach Ram: The autonomy or independence anchor seeks freedom and independence in work. Individuals with this anchor prefer to work at their own pace with their rules through self-employment or freelancing.

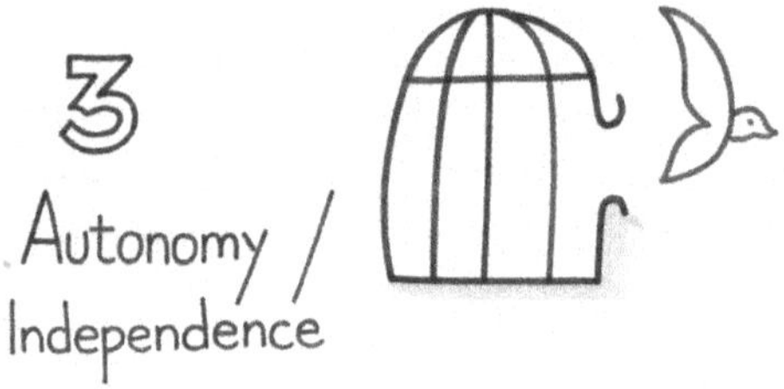

Piyush: So, they prefer having control over their work and schedule?

Coach Ram: Let's look at Maya, a graphic designer with a strong autonomy or independence anchor. Maya is drawn to the creative arts. She likes to express herself through her designs. Rather than work for a traditional design agency, Maya decided to freelance. She wanted the flexibility to choose projects that aligned with her artistic vision. People with an autonomy or independence anchor thrive in workplaces where they have the flexibility to set their own goals and priorities.

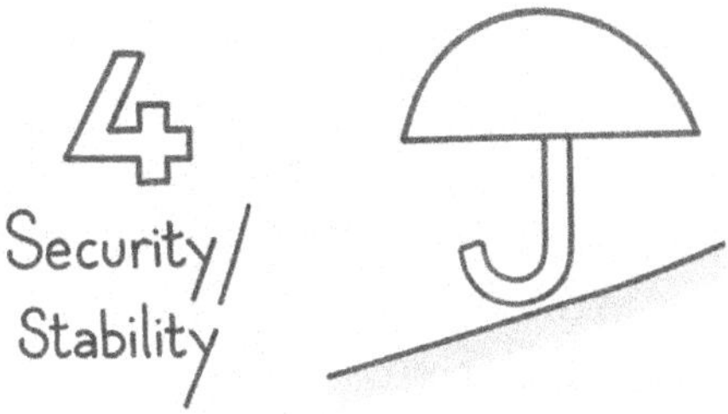

Next, we'll explore the security or stability anchor. This anchor reflects a need for stability and continuity in one's career. Shall we dive into it?

Piyush: Absolutely, I'm curious.

Coach Ram: So, individuals anchored in security or stability are reluctant to take career risks. They prefer streamlined, structured processes. Chaos and frequent changes set them off. They work well in predictable environments which have fixed working processes and expectations.

Piyush: How does this anchor influence their career decisions?

Coach Ram: I know of a finance professional with a strong security or stability anchor. He had a family to support. So, he valued financial security. He always sought roles in established companies. He prioritized benefits like healthcare coverage and retirement plans. Peace of mind motivates him, not the desire to surpass others. Also, as you know I have worked in big organizations and small-scale startups. I have noticed a huge difference in the stability that these two work environments offer. Startups have evolving processes. There is a lot of improvement going on. Big organizations have streamlined established processes. I preferred change for its newness and thrill. However, this may not appeal to someone who has a stability or security anchor.

Piyush: That makes sense. What about the next anchor?

Coach Ram: The next anchor is entrepreneurial creativity. Individuals with this anchor want to create new businesses. At their workplace, these individuals want to solve problems. They thrive on innovation and risks. They pursue personal gain and recognition for their accomplishments.

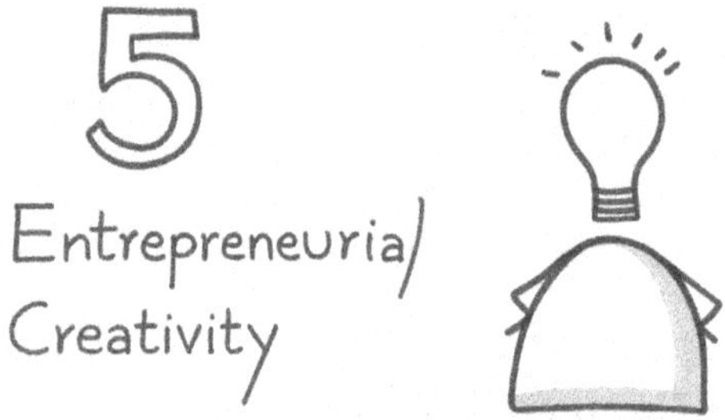

Now, I am keen to tell you about the next anchor.

The service or dedication to a cause anchor focuses on serving others. A desire to make a positive impact on people motivates these individuals. Can you think of any other nuances?

Piyush: These individuals could sacrifice higher salaries or promotions. For them, serving a cause outweighs any personal rewards.

Coach Ram: Correct! Now, the next anchor is a pure challenge. Individuals with this anchor are driven to tackle difficult problems. They thrive on competition and achievement.

Piyush: So, they're focused on pushing their limits?

Coach Ram: Let's talk about Rohan, an athlete with a strong pure challenge anchor. Rohan is drawn to sports that test his physical and mental limits such as marathons, running, and rock climbing. He thrives on the rush of competition and a new challenge. Whether it's training

for an endurance race or a difficult climb, Rohan finds satisfaction in pushing himself and achieving impossible feats.

Piyush: I understand. What about the lifestyle anchor?

Coach Ram: The lifestyle anchor is about balancing work with family, leisure, and other personal pursuits. The goal is to achieve harmony. Professionals motivated by the lifestyle anchor may choose flexible hours or remote work with generous vacation time to feel fulfilled.

Piyush: It's fascinating to learn about these different career anchors and how they shape people's career choices. Thank you for explaining these anchors in detail. It's been incredibly insightful. I'm intrigued by the concept of career anchors. How do you think someone can identify their dominant career anchor?

Coach Ram: Identifying your dominant career anchor requires introspection. One approach is to reflect on past experiences and consider what aspects of your work have brought you fulfillment. You can also think about the values and priorities that guide your career decisions. Additionally, there are online assessments that can help you uncover your career anchors through structured exercises and questionnaires.

Piyush: That makes sense. Once someone identifies their dominant career anchor, how can they leverage it to make better career decisions?

Coach Ram: Leveraging your dominant career anchor involves aligning your career choices and goals with your core values and motivations. For example, if you discover that your anchor is entrepreneurial creativity, you may seek opportunities that allow you to innovate and take risks. For example, you could start your business or pursue roles in dynamic and innovative emerging industries. By understanding and honoring your career anchor, you can make decisions that align with your passions and strengths. Ultimately, this would lead to fulfillment and success in your career.

Piyush: That sounds like a valuable tool for career planning. Are there any challenges or pitfalls that people should be aware of when exploring their career anchors?

Coach Ram: Absolutely, Piyush. Anchors can provide insights into our motivations and preferences but career paths are rarely linear or static. People's priorities and interests can evolve with time. Our dominant anchor may change as we gain new experiences and perspectives. Additionally, we may encounter external factors such as economic changes or industry trends that may impact our career trajectories. It's essential to approach career planning with an openness to change. We must allow ourselves the freedom to explore new opportunities and adapt to shifting circumstances.

Coach Ram and Piyush parted ways. After this exchange, Piyush took the first step towards self-discovery. We will revisit Piyush's self-exploration in a while.

Self-Reflective Questionnaire

1. What is your preferred career path? Are you drawn to the traditional climb of the linear path, the mastery of the expert trajectory, the lateral dance of the spiral trajectory, or the adventurous exploration of the transitory route? Your answer is the key to unlocking a path that aligns with your unique aspirations.
2. You can explore assessments to understand your career anchors. Remember that your career trek is not set in stone—it is a canvas waiting for your brushstrokes, an evolving narrative shaped by your choices.

Careertrek
#CoachRam
Which are your top 3 anchors ?

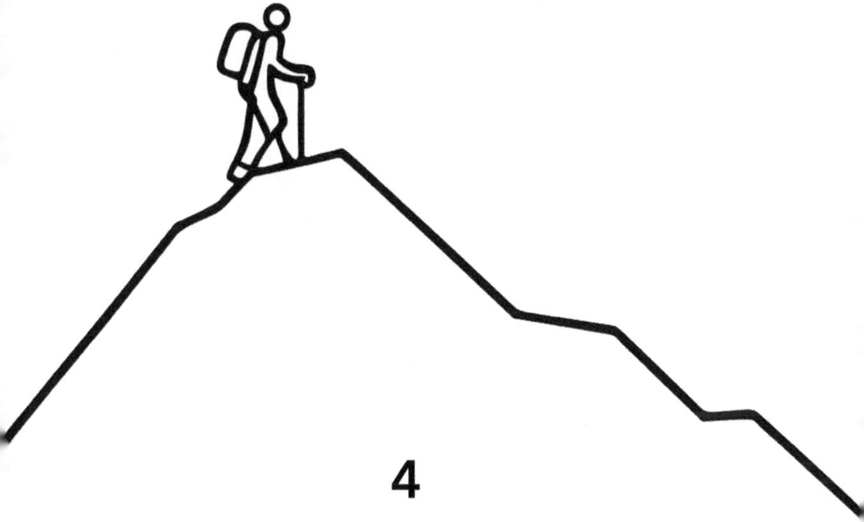

4

Do You Have Your PBOD?

Set up your personal board of directors to guide your career out of the rut

A company needs leadership to achieve its goals. Think of a CEO or a board of directors who make the right decisions and plans to guide their ship. We are no different. Our career trek, like any journey, requires navigation and guidance. In this chapter, we'll explore how we can support ourselves with a personal board of directors (PBOD).

Self-Reflective Questionnaire

1. Have you sought career guidance and not received it?
2. Do you have a mentor or a sponsor outside your current organization?
3. Have you ever considered building your personal board of directors (PBOD)?

Piyush and Coach Ram met over a cup of coffee. Piyush wanted guidance on the challenges that every decision comes with.

Coach Ram: Piyush, it's good to see you. How's everything going for you?

Piyush: Coach, I'm hitting a roadblock. Every step forward comes with new challenges. I'm not sure how to tackle them.

Coach Ram: Ever thought about having a personal board of directors?

Piyush, you seem puzzled. A personal board of directors, or PBOD for short, represents your dream team. They support your aspirations.

Piyush: How can a PBOD help us?

Coach Ram: They are your squad of advisors. They bring their unique skills and insights. They guide you and challenge your perspectives. They have your back as you as you trek through your professional journey.

Piyush: Like career sherpas helping us navigate the treacherous terrain of corporate life?

Coach Ram: Good analogy! Now, let's break down the roles you need on your PBOD expedition. First up, we've got the Industry Insider. Your go-to guru for industry news. They've got their finger on the pulse of your field. They dish out the latest trends, challenges, and opportunities faster than you can say, "LinkedIn update."

Piyush: So, they can tell me if I should embrace the latest tech trend or stick with the tried-and-true method?

Coach Ram: You got it! Next, we've got the Life Navigator. They know how to navigate corporate chaos.

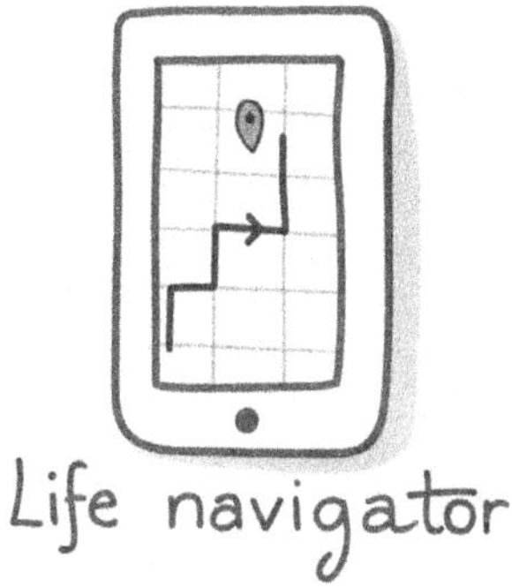

Piyush: Got it. And then there's the Cheerleader.

Coach Ram: Bingo! They are rooting for your success like a die-hard fan at a sports game. They're the wind beneath your wings, the pep in your step, the... well, you get the idea?

Cheerleader

Piyush: So, they're like my motivator?

Coach Ram: Exactly! Now, brace yourself for the next one: The Constructive Critic.

Constructive critic

Piyush: Sounds intimidating.

Coach Ram: Nah, they're not as scary as they sound. They're like the tough-love aunt or uncle who's not afraid to tell you when you've got spinach in your teeth or when your PowerPoint presentation is a snoozefest. But hey, their feedback is gold for your growth.

Piyush: Fair enough. And then there's the Leadership Figure.

Coach Ram: You got it. They're the seasoned pro who's been there and done that. They have the corner office to prove it. They're like Yoda to Luke Skywalker, guiding you toward greatness.

Piyush: And what about Generational Voices?

Coach Ram: They are the ones who keep you young at heart while also dropping serious wisdom bombs. They're—the Gen Z TikTok influencer meets the Baby Boomer CEO—offering a perfect blend of modern insights and timeless advice. For example, a CEO of 40+ years having a 20- or 30-year-old in their PBOD for advice.

Piyush: Sounds like a diverse crew. And what about the Connector?

Coach Ram: They're the social butterflies of your PBOD. They'll connect you with important people faster than a networking event. Also, Piyush, you should know that when we have mentors and sponsors, we are more likely to be successful.

Piyush: That's great, Coach Ram. It aligns with what we've been talking about. But can you explain more about the differences between mentors and sponsors?

Coach Ram: Of course. Mentors provide guidance, advice, and support based on their experience. They help you navigate your career, develop your skills, and offer insights into your professional growth. A mentor might help you identify your strengths, work on your weaknesses, and offer advice on career decisions.

Sponsors are the senior staff within your organization or industry who actively advocate for you. They use their influence and network to open doors for you, recommend you for opportunities, and help you advance in your career. While mentors provide guidance, sponsors promote your career.

Piyush: That makes sense.

Coach Ram: Mentors and sponsors are crucial for career development. Their roles are different. Mentors can be internal or external to your organization. They usually focus on your personal and professional growth. Sponsors, however, are often from within your organization. They are in positions where they can influence decisions and create opportunities for you.

Piyush: Can you give me some examples of how mentors and sponsors have helped people in their careers?

Coach Ram: Certainly. Let's talk about Dhriti again. At the digital marketing startup where Dhriti worked, she had a mentor named Priya. Priya guided Dhriti on how to develop her skills in different areas of content writing, advised her on career decisions, and helped her build her confidence. This mentorship enabled Dhriti to gain a variety of opportunities and helped her progress in her career.

When Dhriti joined the company she currently works at, she had a sponsor named Rakesh. Rakesh, a senior executive, advocated for Dhriti because he noticed her potential. He recommended her for high-profile projects and job promotions. Dhriti advanced quickly within the company. She took on more significant roles and responsibilities.

Piyush: It seems like having both mentors and sponsors can provide a well-rounded support system for career growth.

Coach Ram: Absolutely. Mentors help you build the foundation of your career, while sponsors help you climb the ladder. Identify individuals who can offer guidance and those who can advocate for you. Building these relationships takes time and effort, but the benefits are tremendous.

Piyush: How do I go about finding a mentor or a sponsor?

Coach Ram: Identify your goals and areas where you need guidance or support. For mentors, approach people you respect and admire with the type of career you want for yourself. Ask if they would be willing to mentor you. Be clear about what you're looking for. Tell them how they can help you.

For sponsors, focus on building relationships with senior leaders in your organization. Demonstrate your value through your work. Be proactive in seeking opportunities and let them see your potential. Sponsors could emerge from these relationships when they notice your dedication and potential.

Piyush: I'll find opportunities to connect with potential mentors and sponsors.

Piyush: So, how do I build my PBOD? Seems overwhelming.

Coach Ram: It's simpler than you think, Piyush. Find folks who naturally align with your career goals and values. Be clear about what you expect from them. Don't forget about reciprocity. Remember, it's a potluck dinner—everyone brings something to the table.

Piyush: I need to assemble my dream team of career advisors. Keep the communication flowing. Show my appreciation for receiving help.

Coach Ram: You got it, Piyush. Now, conquer the corporate wilderness with your PBOD by your side! I want to talk about nurturing your PBOD relationships.

Piyush: Right, maintaining those connections is key. But how do I keep the flame alive with each member of my PBOD?

Coach Ram: Great question, my friend. Schedule regular check-ins with each member. Whether it's a monthly coffee chat or a quarterly Zoom call. Update them about your career. Ask for their input on key decisions.

Coach Ram: Now let's find out how to make the most out of your PBOD.

Remember to check in with them at regular intervals for advice and career updates.

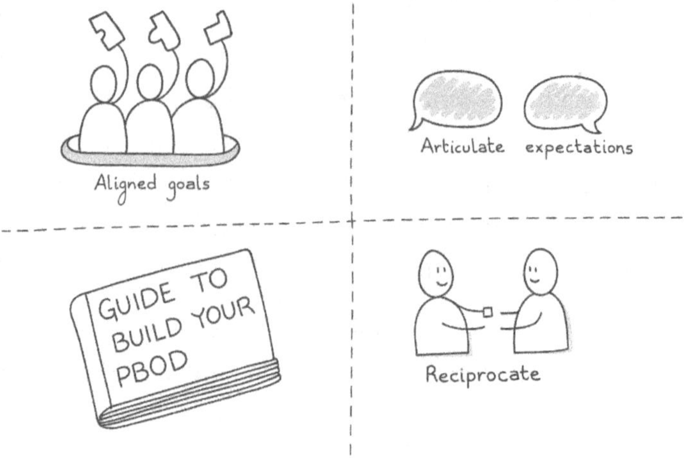

Piyush: So, staying connected is key. What else should we keep in mind?

Coach Ram: Here's a nugget of wisdom: Don't be that person who only reaches out when they need something. Don't look opportunistic.

Piyush: Makes sense. How can we foster meaningful conversations with our PBOD members?

Coach Ram: Openness is key. Be willing to share your thoughts and listen to their feedback. Remember, it's a two-way street. Don't forget to circle back. Let them know how their advice has helped you. Reciprocate.

Piyush: Great point, Coach Ram. It's important to show our appreciation for their guidance. But what about giving back to them?

Coach Ram: Spot on. Be ready to lend a helping hand to your PBOD members whenever they need it. Make introductions, assist with projects, or offer any other support. Be there for them just as they are for you.

Piyush: And one more thing, Coach Ram. Should we consider being someone else's PBOD?

Coach Ram: Absolutely. Sharing your knowledge and offering guidance and support to others in their career journeys can be rewarding. It's about paying it forward and building a network of allies.

Piyush: Thank you, Coach. I'll put your insights into practice.

Coach Ram: Building and nurturing your PBOD is like tending to a garden. With your care and attention, it will flourish and bear fruit in your professional journey.

Piyush read articles, attended workshops, filled out questionnaires, and connected with professionals to understand and build his PBOD.

He pondered over the background of his dream team, the type of skills or industry experience they needed to have to guide him toward success. Piyush realized he couldn't just wish for his dream team to appear. He needed to find them. He attended industry events, joined professional networks, and reached out to individuals who could play key roles in his career advancement.

Piyush's effort to seek career guidance proved his commitment to success.

Self-Coaching Questions

1. What criteria will you use to select individuals for your personal board of directors?
2. What events or online platforms would you sign up to, to find your mentors and sponsors?

Remember that building a PBOD and actively finding mentors and sponsors are pivotal for a successful career. Take charge. Feel fulfilled.

Here's a chart to help you design your PBOD. List three people who fit each category of the PBOD:

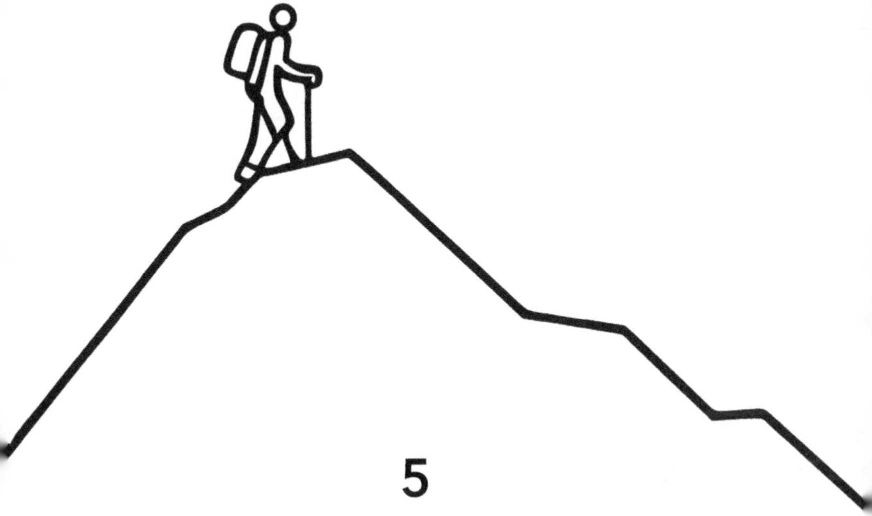

5

Derailers and Drivers for Growth

Factors that can make or break your career

Are you a rising star, climbing the corporate ladder with the world at your feet? It's a common narrative. Yet, the truth is, not everyone reaches the top. Less than a third of high-potential individuals succeed; the rest derail or stagnate. A train can unexpectedly come off its tracks to a halt, and so too can our careers. Leaders often hit plateaus due to a significant flaw or weakness, i.e., derailers that hinder their progress to a downfall.

A derailer is a flaw that blocks an individual from reaching their potential. It can become a fatal flaw if left uncorrected. We'll tackle the most common career derailers and how to avoid them.

Through research and self-reflection, Piyush put together a robust PBOD. He crossed milestones in his career trek. Later, he even helped others figure out their career trek. What goes around comes around. It couldn't get better than this right?

Wrong. Despite his guidance, Piyush's advice hit blocks in their careers.

Piyush had lost control over his career trek as well. He would have ended at the bottom if it weren't for the hands that grabbed him right on time—his PBOD.

Piyush remembered that he had watched a YouTube video in which derailers were discussed. Now was the right time to ask his mentor about derailers in detail.

Self-Reflective Questionnaire

1. How do you react to criticism? Are you open to self-reflection or do you resist it?
2. Assess your adaptability to change. Reflect on a situation where you faced significant change in the workplace. How did you respond? Was it a smooth experience or a challenging one?

These questions aim to help you identify your strengths and your limitations.

In the conversation below, Coach Ram sheds light on the pitfalls derailing our progress and the skills required to thrive in today's dynamic work environment.

Coach Ram: Piyush, navigating our career is like walking a tightrope, balancing confidence with aggression, openness with apathy, and charisma with manipulation.

Piyush: That is quite a challenge. How do people manage to stay on track without veering off course?

Coach Ram: Self-awareness is key. Many people sabotage their careers unknowingly, despite being smart and capable because they lack self-awareness.

Piyush: Really? How does that happen?

Coach Ram: Imagine this: someone thinks they know everything. They take control of every situation. They shut down other people's ideas and alienate their colleagues. They want to be the smartest person in the room but they come off as arrogant instead.

Piyush: I see what you mean. They are in their bubble and don't see how their actions affect others.

Coach Ram: Exactly! And then some people shut down any new ideas with a "No" or "But." They're not open to different perspectives. This attitude can hinder progress.

Piyush: That doesn't seem productive.

Coach Ram: Yes. And let's not forget about negative people. They bring down the mood with their pessimism. Nobody wants to work with a Debbie Downer, am I right?

Piyush: Absolutely, Coach. Positivity is important in the workplace.

Coach Ram: And then there's the blame game. Some people can't admit their mistakes and instead shift the blame to others. This behavior can damage trust.

Piyush: It sounds like humility is key to avoiding these pitfalls.

Coach Ram: You got it. And speaking of pitfalls, bullying, and emotional volatility are a no-no in any professional setting. Nobody wants to work with a bull in a china shop.

Piyush: That's a vivid image, Coach.

Coach Ram: To summarize, be open to feedback, admit mistakes, and seek self-improvement. It's like driving—you've got to keep your eyes on the road and adjust to the changing environment.

Piyush, still processing the career derailers, leaned in with a furrowed brow. "Coach Ram," he said, "This feels like navigating a minefield blindfolded. How do I avoid these career landmines?"

Coach Ram: Identifying the landmines is half the battle won. Some of the derailers are common and fatal for your career. The famous HR consulting firm Korn Ferry has published extensive research on this. Let's address them one by one.

The first derailer is unawareness. When you can't see yourself as you are. You might overestimate your strengths and underestimate your weaknesses. Self-awareness is crucial for growth, and without it, you risk derailment.

Piyush: I can see how that would be a problem. What's next?

Coach Ram: The second derailer is rigidity—resisting change and struggling outside your comfort zone. You struggle with adapting to change, whether there's a new boss, process, technology, or strategy. Flexibility is key in today's fast-paced world. Being rigid can hold you back.

Piyush: Adaptability is important. What else can derail us?

Coach Ram: The third is disorganization. If you let things fall through the cracks, overcommit, and under-deliver, miss key details, you'll be seen as unreliable. This behavior can derail your career quickly.

Piyush: That makes sense. Being organized is crucial for maintaining trust and reliability. What's the fourth derailer?

Coach Ram: The fourth is arrogance—when you say one thing and do another, break confidences, and gossip about others. Arrogance is damaging to your reputation and relationships.

Piyush: Arrogance can alienate people. What's the fifth derailer?

Coach Ram: The fifth derailer is cracking under pressure—when you can't handle stress, become emotional and unpredictable, or even hostile towards others, your performance suffers.

Piyush: Handling stress is important for any job. What about the sixth derailer?

Coach Ram: The sixth is defensiveness. If you can't take criticism, deny mistakes, blame others, and the messenger, you miss out on opportunities to learn and improve.

Piyush: I can see how being defensive would be a barrier to growth. What's next?

Coach Ram: The seventh derailer is not being a team player. If you don't pull together with others, don't share credit for success, and undermine team spirit, you create a toxic work environment.

Piyush: Teamwork is so important. What about the eighth derailer?

Coach Ram: The eighth derailer is hearing but not listening. You might hear others, but you don't listen. You appear insensitive, unaware, or apathetic about the impact of what you say and do to others. It leads to poor interpersonal skills because you never ask about others or show genuine interest in their perspectives.

Piyush: Listening is crucial for good communication. What's the ninth derailer?

Coach Ram: The ninth derailer is poor performance—being inconsistent in meeting targets and objectives, procrastinating, and lacking experience and expertise.

Piyush: Performance is obviously key to career advancement. What's the tenth derailer?

Coach Ram: The tenth derailer is lack of independence. If you stay with the same boss or mentor for too long and have difficulty handling challenging assignments without help, you're not demonstrating your ability to be self-sufficient.

Piyush: Independence shows that you can manage responsibilities on your own. What's the eleventh derailer?

Coach Ram: The eleventh one is over-reliance on one skill. If you're a one-trick pony, using the same talent, function, or technology, and act as if one talent alone is sufficient, you limit your growth and versatility.

Piyush: Versatility is important for adapting to new roles and challenges. What's the last derailer?

Coach Ram: The twelfth derailer is poor interpersonal skills—when you have difficulty interacting with others and your miscommunication leads to strained relationships. Interpersonal skills are essential to build a supportive network and collaborate successfully.

Coach Ram: Being mindful of these derailers and working to avoid them can help you stay on track in your career. Be open to learning, be flexible, and develop your personal and professional skills.

Piyush: That's a lot. Avoiding these derailers requires a lot of self-awareness and adaptability.

Coach Ram: Exactly, Piyush. Next, we'll delve into the components that can guarantee you success. These drivers are **ABCDEF**: Antifragility, Business Acumen, Communication, Digital Mindset, Empathy, and Fire in the Belly, a.k.a., passion or ambition.

Piyush: I'm intrigued, Coach. Tell me more about these drivers.

Coach Ram: Sure. Let's start with Antifragility. It's about growing stronger through challenges like muscles do under strain. You face setbacks, learn, adapt, and become stronger.

Antifragility means seeing problems as opportunities to improve and build your strengths. This mindset helps you thrive in your career.

Piyush: Got it. What about Business Acumen?

Coach Ram: Business Acumen is about understanding the business side of things—knowing how companies operate and making decisions that benefit the organization. Being hands-on with the business and understanding the bigger picture.

Piyush: So, it's about being aware of how businesses work and making smart decisions?

Coach Ram: Yes. When you understand the business landscape, you become an asset because you can align your work with the company's goals.

Piyush: That makes sense. What's next?

Coach Ram: Communication is crucial; conveying your ideas clearly and building relationships shouldn't be overlooked. Good communication helps you feel understood and connected with your colleagues, collaborate, and lead them.

Piyush: Got it. And Digital Mindset?

Coach Ram: Digital Mindset is about being eager to work with technology and explore the various tools and trends. Staying updated with technology helps you work efficiently and keeps you competitive. The competition is between people embracing technology and those avoiding or catching up with technology.

Have you embraced Gen AI tools in your work yet?

Piyush: Huh? And what about the next driver, Empathy?

Coach Ram: Empathy is crucial for leadership. It helps you understand others' feelings, build teamwork, and become a compassionate leader.

Piyush: And could you explain the last driver, Fire in the Belly?

Coach Ram: Fire in the Belly is about passion and ambition. The drive that keeps you going, even when the going gets tough. It's your motivation to achieve your goals.

Piyush: So, it's about having a strong desire to succeed?

Coach Ram: Exactly. It's about being enthusiastic and determined. When you have that fire, you're willing to put in the effort and overcome any obstacle.

Piyush: I'm aware of some of these drivers, Coach Ram, but I have never really thought about them as a set of tools to help me succeed in my career.

Self-Coaching Questions

Antifragility:

- Can you recall a situation where embracing uncertainty at work led to positive outcomes?
- In what ways can you intentionally expose yourself to controlled challenges for personal and professional growth?

Business Acumen:

- How well do you understand the key drivers of success in your current organization or industry or field?
- What steps can you take to enhance your knowledge of market trends, competitor landscapes, and industry dynamics?
- Are there areas in your organization's strategy where you could contribute more effectively with improved business acumen?

Communication:

- Reflect on your recent interactions at work. How effectively do you convey your ideas and listen to others?
- Can you recall a situation where miscommunication led to challenges? How else do you think you could have communicated your message in a way that you felt understood?

- What steps can you take to improve your verbal, written, and non-verbal communication skills?

Digital Mindset:

- Are you comfortable with adapting to new technologies and digital tools in your work?
- Can you identify areas where embracing a digital mindset could streamline your workflow or enhance your productivity?
- What specific skills or knowledge gaps do you need to address to stay relevant in a rapidly evolving digital landscape?

Empathy:

- How well do you understand and consider the perspectives and feelings of your colleagues?
- Are there instances where a lack of empathy may have impacted team cohesion or collaboration?
- What strategies can you employ to cultivate a more empathetic approach in your professional relationships?

Fire in the Belly:

- Reflect on your goals and see if they belong to the Big Hairy Audacious Goals category (BHAG).

THE DERAILERS & DRIVERS FOR SUCCESS
#untrustworthy
#disorganised
#unaware
#arrogant
#rigid
#crack under pressure
#fire in the belly
#empathy
#not a team player
#Poor performance
#not listening
#defensive
#dependent
#digital mindset
#over reliant
#business acumen
Communication
#antifragility

#Careertrek
#Coachram

6

Managing Professional Relationships

Build win-win relationships at work

Professional relationships drive collaboration and productivity. When trust and open communication exist, they create a fertile ground for teamwork, problem-solving, and the execution of projects. Ideas flow, challenges are faced as a team, and innovation blooms.

Healthy relationships at work can lower stress and increase happiness. When we feel supported and appreciated, we're more likely to do our best.

In this chapter, we delve into the art of building relationships at work, handling office politics, and dealing with workplace bullies.

Self-Reflective Questionnaire

1. Envision the values that would define your ideal workplace. How can you apply these values to your current professional relationships?
2. Assess your impact on others. Are you fostering a positive environment, or is there room for improvement?
3. How do you navigate office politics while staying true to your values and building positive relationships with peers?

4. What strategies do you use to handle workplace bullying, and how do these strategies affect your mental and emotional well-being?
5. How do you manage conflicts at the workplace and build relationships with your colleagues?

Even the best professionals can struggle with career progress if they focus only on work skills. One crucial skill often overlooked is people skills.

Your daily interactions with your colleagues, juniors, superiors, and people with the same level of experience as yours have a significant impact on your professional growth.

Piyush was now a senior executive at work, facing new challenges. He struggled to manage the employees he was supposed to lead. Those who held senior positions within the company were not pleased with him. He also noticed a surge in office gossip about him and his colleagues.

With the gossip, his peace of mind was disturbed. His perception of his colleagues was skewed. At times, he acted on these rumors without checking the facts. The office politics, now clear to him, clouded his judgment and led to frequent disputes.

The workplace was no longer healthy. The atmosphere was tense with slander and subtle putdowns. Agitated, Piyush called Coach Ram for advice.

Piyush: "Coach, I've been thinking that success isn't just about being good at your job. It's also about not stepping on too many toes while climbing the ladder. Got any tricks up your sleeve for that?"

Coach Ram: "Office relationships are key. I get what might be bothering you. Think of work relationships like tending a garden. You plant seeds of trust, water them with communication, and hope that your colleagues don't have green thumbs for drama."

Piyush: "But what about office politics? How do we maneuver it? It feels like trying to outsmart a chess grandmaster sometimes."

Coach Ram chuckled, "It's not about dodging politics. Play nice. Be diplomatic. Know who's who, make friends in high places, and keep your moral compass pointing north. And remember, don't sell your soul for the corner office."

He added, "Be savvy, but not slimy. Form alliances based on shared interests and always deliver on your promises. Your street cred is your best defense against office drama."

Piyush's brows furrowed. "And what about workplace bullies?"

Coach Ram sent Piyush an article from *CNBC* by psychologist Tessa West based on her book, *Jerks at Work,* which summarizes as follows: In workplaces, where a significant portion of our lives unfolds, some individuals can cast a shadow on our emotional well-being. Navigating through these challenging situations requires a nuanced understanding of the motivations driving their actions. By identifying distinct behavioral patterns, you can empower yourself with strategies to shield yourself against the draining influence of these office jerks.

One prevalent type is the Kiss-Up/Kick-Downer. These individuals ascend the professional ladder by any means necessary, even resorting to sabotaging colleagues. This is recognizable through behaviors like belittling in front of superiors or offering favors to overwhelmed bosses. Dealing with them involves seeking allies for a reality check and approaching superiors with detailed evidence.

Another toxic archetype is the Gaslighter—master manipulators who weave grand lies to deceive and isolate their victims. With these types, vigilance is crucial, with the need to document instances that feel off and gradually rebuild social networks.

The Credit Stealer operates stealthily, portraying camaraderie while betraying trust by taking credit for others' ideas. To counter this, becoming a trusted advisor to your boss, ensuring everyone's voice is heard in meetings, and defining roles before projects can help mitigate the impact of credit stealers.

In the workplace jungle, the Bulldozer dominates

through assertiveness and expertise. Strategies to handle bulldozers include speaking early in meetings, informing superiors about their dominance, and fostering solutions that involve everyone, including the assertive colleague.

Micromanagers are another breed, drowning employees in trivial tasks and unreasonable urgency. Coping mechanisms involve discussing overarching goals, establishing clear expectations, and engaging in short, frequent meetings for effective communication.

The Neglectful Boss operates in cycles of long periods of neglect followed by sudden control. Strategies include scheduling meetings to address needs, assuming smaller tasks to assist the boss, and seeking expertise from alternative sources.

Lastly, the Free Rider excels in doing minimal work while reaping undeserved rewards. Integrating fairness checks, highlighting their value to the team without accusations, and setting boundaries are essential strategies to neutralize the impact of Free Riders.

In office dynamics, understanding and effectively countering these various office jerks can significantly contribute to a healthier, more productive work environment.

Piyush was overwhelmed with more questions. "Coach Ram, it's like walking a tightrope. How do you stay true to yourself without stepping on any toes?"

Coach Ram replied, "Authenticity is your secret sauce. Stick to your guns, even when the going gets tough.

Whom Have You Met Today?
#careertrek
#coachram
Kiss-up kick downer
micro manager
I am Important
bulldozer
gaslighter
NO!
neglectful boss
> work rewards
free rider
other People's work
Credit Stealer

People respect honesty more than a smooth-talking salesman."

Piyush nodded, "But what if being authentic means rubbing the boss the wrong way?"

Coach Ram grinned, "The eternal struggle. Adapt, Piyush, but don't lose yourself in the process. Find common ground where you can be yourself without raising too many eyebrows. It's a dance, not a battlefield. Once I had to face a situation where I had to contradict my boss. I explained my stance to my boss in a non-confrontational tone and also told him that I will toe the line if he still is not convinced."

Piyush decided to dive back into his work with renewed vigor. He was determined to tackle challenges with a fresh perspective, approach interactions with new-found empathy, and navigate office politics with humor and wit.

A couple of days later, Coach Ram and Piyush reconnected over a phone call.

Coach Ram: "You know, Piyush, there are a lot of myths floating around about office politics."

Piyush was intrigued. "Myths? Like what?"

Coach Ram nodded knowingly. "Well, for starters, some folks think you can't be a good person if you play office politics. But that's hogwash. You can still be ethical while using politics to understand what makes your colleagues tick."

Piyush scratched his head. “But can’t you just avoid office politics altogether?”

Coach Ram chuckled. “Wouldn’t that be nice? But nope, politics is like those pesky pigeons in the park. They’re everywhere, even in places you would least expect to find them.”

Piyush’s eyes widened. “Really? But I thought if you work hard, politics won’t affect your career.”

Coach Ram: “Wishful thinking, my friend. Hard work is important but if you don’t toot your own horn occasionally, nobody will know about your accomplishments.”

Piyush: “And what about remote work? Does that make office politics disappear?”

Coach Ram smirked. “Not a chance. Even with everyone working from home, office politics was alive and kicking. They’ve just gone virtual with Zoom calls instead of water cooler gossip.”

Piyush frowned, “But isn’t being politically savvy something you’re born with?”

Coach Ram shook his head adamantly. “Nah, that’s just a myth. Anyone can learn the ropes of office politics with practice and intention. It’s like riding a bike; you keep at it until you get the hang of it. Still, there are some actions you can take to navigate office politics effectively. First off, it’s important to change how you see office politics. Don’t think of it as something negative but a way to build relationships that can provide favorable outcomes for you.”

Piyush noted the advice. "So, it's all about building relationships?"

Coach Ram: "Observe and adapt. Invest in relationships, including with those who don't always agree with you. Avoid office gossip. It might seem harmless, but it can create rifts and damage relationships."

Piyush nodded in agreement. "Got it, Coach. No gossiping."

Coach Ram continued, "Avoid talking about others behind their backs. Ensure what you're saying about anyone is something you'd be comfortable saying to their face. This will ensure you can be authentic and you are not second guessing yourself when you are talking to someone else. Being authentic will free you from all awkward scenarios at work."

Piyush understood the importance of integrity in communication.

"Makes sense, Coach. I'll keep that in mind."

"Good. Now, let's talk about how to handle interactions with your superiors. Avoid flattery; bosses can see through that. Instead, focus on adding value to conversations and making them feel appreciated without buttering them up."

Piyush leaned in, eager to learn more. "How can I do that, Coach?"

Coach Ram continued, "Listen, contribute meaningfully by creating impact, and offer constructive suggestions. Show initiative by taking on challenging tasks and solving problems. By demonstrating your competence and dedication, you'll naturally catch your superiors' attention and earn their respect."

Piyush felt confident about navigating interactions with his superiors using Coach Ram's guiding tools.

Coach Ram continued, "You know, Piyush, a big issue in workplaces today is this obsession with individual achievements. Everyone is trying to win a solo race in a team sport! In an organization, the goals are defined with an individual focus and collaborative behavior takes the backseat. Personal disputes, politics, etc., are an outcome of this mindset."

Piyush: "Coach, what makes a good work relationship last?"

Coach Ram replied, "Piyush, you're diving into the deep end now! Let's start with trust. Trust is like the glue that holds a relationship together. When you trust your team, you can relax knowing they've your back. There's no need to peek over your shoulder! In a healthy workplace, everyone's opinions are valued—a big brainstorming session where every idea gets a chance to shine. Respect is the secret sauce that makes teamwork delicious!"

Piyush chuckled at the analogy. "I like that, Coach."

Coach Ram: "Glad you approve, Piyush! Now, onto self-awareness. Own up to your mistakes and take responsibility for your actions. Don't blame others or throw tantrums. Only toddlers do that!"

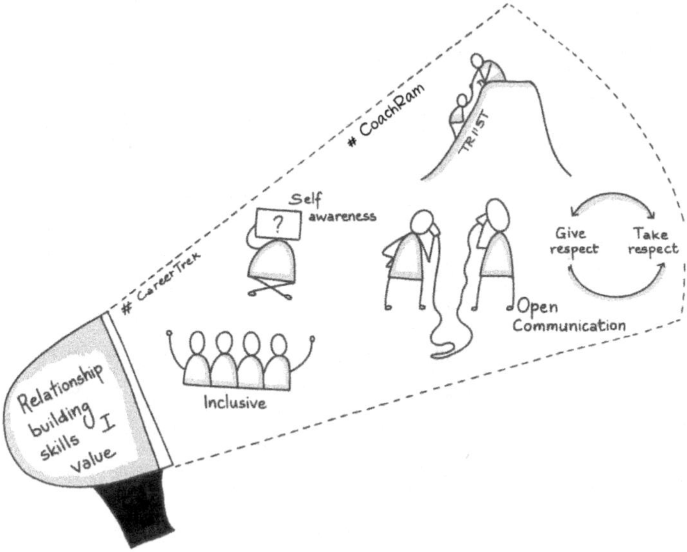

Piyush laughed, picturing a grown adult having a tantrum in the office. "I don't want to be that guy!"

Coach Ram nodded, "Exactly! And speaking of grown-ups, let's talk about inclusion. It's not only about tolerating differences but celebrating them, too. Like a potluck where everyone brings their dish, diversity makes the workplace feast more flavorful!"

Piyush grinned, "Potluck of perspectives, I like it!"

Coach Ram chuckled, "You catch on quick, Piyush! And lastly, open communication. It's the lifeline of any relationship. No secrets, no hidden agendas. Just straight-up honesty, whether it's through emails, texts, or good old face-to-face chats."

Piyush: "Coach, I understand that building relationships is important, but what relationships should I focus on?"

"While it's good to be friendly with everyone, there are a few relationships that need TLC," Coach Ram explained.

Piyush asked curiously, "What do you mean by TLC?"

Coach Ram explained, "TLC stands for Tender Loving Care. It means giving extra attention to certain relationships. For example, your relationship with your boss. Make sure you're clear about their expectations and give them regular updates on your progress. Or your relationships with key colleagues. Collaborate with them on projects and support each other."

Piyush nodded, thinking about his team. "Got it, Coach. I'll focus on building trust, showing respect, being self-aware, celebrating diversity, and keeping communication open. And I'll give extra attention to important relationships."

Coach Ram smiled, "That's the spirit, Piyush! Remember, strong work relationships make the job more enjoyable and help you succeed. Keep working on these aspects, and you'll see the positive impact on your career."

Piyush was eager to learn more.

Coach Ram spoke after taking a pause, "Your relationship with your boss is key. They've got a big impact on your work life, you know? They can make or break your career!"

Piyush agreed, "So, how can I make sure my relationship with the boss is solid?"

Coach Ram: "Schedule regular one-on-one chats with your boss. It's your chance to show them what you're made of, how you're adding value to the team."

Piyush took note of the advice, "Got it, regular chats with the boss!"

Coach Ram: "Now, maintaining the relationship managing upwards is another ball game. It's like figuring out how your boss likes their coffee—you must tailor your approach to fit their style! Next, your relationships with stakeholders. These are the folks who have a stake in your success like customers and suppliers. You must keep them happy, too! You must figure out what you need from them and what they need from you. It's like drawing a treasure map—you must know where you're headed!"

"Then there's emotional intelligence—understanding your own emotions and being able to read the room. Developing your EI makes you a relationship ninja."

Piyush reminded himself to work on his EI.

"Listening is key, too," Coach Ram emphasized. "People love it when you pay attention to the details when they tell you something and ask questions. It's like giving them a warm hug with your ears."

"And don't forget to schedule time for building relationships," Coach Ram added. "Even if it's just a quick coffee or a small act of kindness, those little moments add up."

Piyush understood the importance of making time for connections.

"Lastly," Coach Ram said, "Be positive and avoid gossip like the plague. Positivity is like sunshine—it brightens everyone's day."

Piyush: "Makes sense, Coach."

Coach Ram: "Sometimes, even a relationship that used to be all sunshine and rainbows could turn stormy. When that happens, it's time to reflect on the good times. Remembering those positive moments can help smooth things over."

Piyush scribbled notes, his mind already wandering to past conflicts.

"But," Coach Ram continued, "If the relationship is rough, it might be time to take a good, hard look in the mirror. Negative feelings can make us act out, so stop them in their tracks. Lastly, find some common ground. If you're butting heads with someone, figure out what you both want and work towards it together."

Self-Coaching Questions

Reflection on Relationships:

- What's your most enjoyable relationship at work? Are there relationships that cause you stress?
- Reflect on how your own actions or perspectives could be affecting those work relationships.

Teamwork:

- Think of a misunderstanding that happened with your peer in the past. What could you have done to avoid the situation?
- Were you a mentor or mentee to anyone?
- How would your teammates describe your collaboration style?
- How did you help your teammates achieve their goals? How did you hinder them?

As Piyush reflected on these questions, he realized that building relationships was an art. Only with intention, skill, and continuous effort could he reap the rewards.

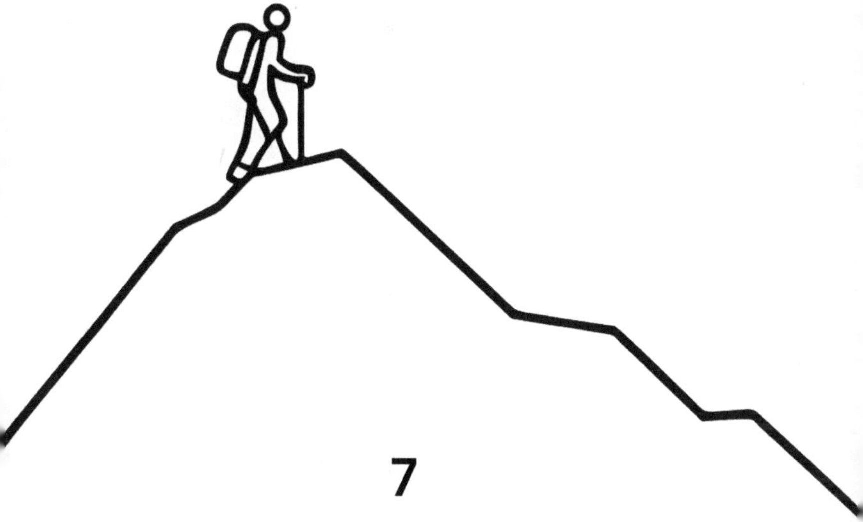

7

Showcasing Impact

Master the art of marketing yourself

Corporates reward those who stand out. If you want the reward, you must demonstrate your uniqueness. Putting yourself out there through your abilities, achievements, or distinct perspective, gets you attention. Remember, what is seen gets sold. Don't be afraid to show off your skills and tell the world what you can offer. The loudest roar gets heard first.

Self-Reflective Questionnaire

1. Do I have beliefs that hinder showcasing my achievements?
2. Do I downplay my achievements or attribute them solely to external factors?
3 How do I feel when receiving positive feedback or recognition for my work? Does it make me uncomfortable or doubtful?
4 Do I dismiss praise when I receive it? Do I overemphasize my mistakes at work? Do I feel like I don't deserve special treatment because I don't have any special skills?
5. What are the moments in my career when I doubted my achievements and capabilities so much so that I missed sharing my opinions and even denied myself opportunities to progress?

With his PBOD supporting him, Piyush made good progress in his career. He is now a senior professional in consulting space for retail.

He recently attended a seminar on careers. He had a lot to take in from the seminar on showcasing impact at work. Here are some thoughts that stood out to him:

So often, it's easy to get lost in the shuffle. We quietly toil away, hoping our hard work will speak for itself. But let's face it, my friend, in a world where success has many friends and failure is an orphan, waiting for your work to be discovered—like a hidden gem in a dusty old warehouse—won't cut it.

You see, the world of work is a complex web of interdependence. Whether you're a part of a team or flying solo, your actions ripple out and affect those around you. And when things go well, everyone wants to claim a piece of the glory. But when they don't, suddenly you're left holding the bag.

And think about the higher-ups—the decision-makers, the bigwigs, the ones with the power to shape your career. They have a lot on their plates, my friend. Between meetings, emails, and emergencies, it's hard for your superiors to keep track of your progress. To get noticed, you have to make some noise.

There are many attention seekers at your workplace clamoring for spotlight. Some of them may talk a big game, but when push comes to shove, they have nothing to back up their claims with. So, speak up about your achievements amid the noise—give them proof, not just empty words.

I know what you're thinking—why should I stoop to their level? Why should I brag about my accomplishments when my work should speak for itself? Well, my friend, it's not bragging; it's standing up and being noticed. It's taking pride in your work and making sure others recognize your value.

Think of it like this: you have a product—a damn good product—sitting in a warehouse gathering dust. Sure, it's great, but if no one knows about it, what good is it? You have to put that product in the showroom, polish it, and let it shine for all to see. Because at the end of the day, if you're not willing to showcase yourself, who else will?

Don't be afraid to toot your own horn. Showcase yourself with pride, but do it with substance.

Piyush was no stranger to success. After you reached a peak, couple of failures make you doubt your entire success story and your capabilities. Piyush hit this zone now. The relentless doubt crept in, triggering what psychologists call "imposter syndrome." Piyush's journey, much like many of us, unfolded as a narrative of triumphs and tribulations against this formidable foe. One day, as Piyush sipped his coffee in the office breakroom, he overheard colleagues discussing their recent accomplishments. Instead of pride, a wave of anxiety swept over him.

Piyush *(whispering to himself):* Do I deserve praise for landing that big client? Maybe it was just luck.

This internal dialogue became a constant companion, surfacing whenever success knocked on Piyush's door. The more he achieved, the louder the voice became, casting shadows over his capabilities.

Amid this negative self-talk, an important question came to his mind: what stops us from showcasing ourselves? Why do we hold back so much? And he knew it was time to approach Coach Ram to discuss the conditioning behind it.

Piyush: Hi Coach, recently, I've been thinking about why many of us have trouble showing who we are to the world. Why are we afraid to stand up for ourselves and take credit for what we can do? We often prefer blending in instead of standing out. What do you think holds us back from stepping into the spotlight, even when we have something good to offer?

Coach Ram: You're right on the mark, Piyush. Many people experience this. A voice keeps telling us that we're not good enough and we're just acting clever. Eventually, we'll get caught. It's the fear of being seen as someone who doesn't fit or doesn't deserve success or praise. This fear often makes us play down our accomplishments, hide our skills, and stay unnoticed to avoid failure or rejection. But Piyush, the imposter syndrome is false. And we can start to get past it once we see it for what it is. We need to remember our worth, connect with supportive people, broaden our views, and break free from the limits we place on ourselves. It's hard but worth it.

Piyush: The imposter syndrome gnaws at me. It makes me doubt my accomplishments and fear being exposed as a fraud, even with proof of my success. How do I deal with that?

Coach Ram: Well, Piyush, know that you're not alone in this struggle. Imposter syndrome is common. Many high-achievers deal with it.

Piyush: That's a little reassuring. But how do I overcome imposter syndrome?

Coach Ram: Through self-reflection. Dig into your beliefs. Who do you think is the pinnacle of success in your organization? What qualities of theirs make them worthy of their success? Why do you think you fall short in comparison? List reasons for your self-doubts.

Confront your thoughts head-on with a journal. Journaling is a trend these days! Write down your achievements—big or small—and revisit them regularly. It's the equivalent of giving yourself a pep talk.

Piyush: What else can I do?

Coach Ram: Networking is a game-changer. I'm not talking about collecting business cards like Pokémon. Network with intent. Surround yourself with supportive people who can offer perspective and encouragement. You might be surprised how many others are grappling with the same feelings.

Piyush: Thanks, Coach. I'll give these strategies a try. Also, can you talk about networking and how it resolves imposter syndrome?

Coach Ram: Interacting with others in your field gives you a sense of where you stand. You see that everyone has their strengths and weaknesses like you. It's like holding a mirror to yourself.

Piyush: So, am I supposed to benchmark myself with others?

Coach Ram: Exactly, Piyush. You might find that your achievements stack up well compared to others. Or you might realize that everyone faces similar challenges, which can be reassuring. Plus, networking exposes you to different ideas and approaches and broadens your perspective.

Piyush: That makes sense. It's like getting a reality check.

Coach Ram: Precisely. And remember, Piyush, it's not about comparing yourself to others to feel superior or inferior. Know that everyone has their journey and their struggles. Networking helps you see that you're not the only one with doubts.

Piyush: Thanks for clarifying, Coach. I'll keep that in mind as I grow my network.

Coach Ram: Anytime, Piyush. Networking with the intent of understanding our similarities is a powerful tool to overcome imposter syndrome. Make connections with an open mind.

Next, Piyush wanted to learn how he could communicate his impact at work in a compelling manner. Coach Ram explored "storytelling."

Piyush: What do you think are the skills required for business storytelling?

Coach Ram: Business storytelling is a powerful tool in the corporate world. It is basically talking business in a way that *sticks.* Instead of dumping data or boring bullet points, you bring your message alive with a story—something real, relatable, and human. It could be a customer win, a challenge you overcame, or even a small team moment that shows a bigger truth. People don't remember numbers, they remember how you made them *feel.* And stories do just that.

Piyush: That makes sense, Coach. What else should I focus on?

Coach Ram: Another critical skill is emotional intelligence, Piyush. Understanding how your story can evoke specific emotions in your audience is key.

Imagine a manager presenting a business update to their team after a tough quarter. The data shows a dip in performance. Now, consider two approaches:

Without Emotional Intelligence:
The manager jumps straight to the numbers: "We missed our targets by 20%. This isn't acceptable. We need to fix this immediately."

The result: The team feels blamed, demoralized, and disengaged.

With Emotional Intelligence + Storytelling:
The manager opens with a story:

"I want to share a quick story. A few years ago, during a similar rough patch, a team I led felt like we were stuck. But instead of focusing only on what went wrong, we took a step back, understood the reasons, and turned things around in the next quarter. I see similar potential here—I know we've worked hard. Let's dig into the story the numbers are telling us and rewrite the next chapter together."

Piyush: I can see how emotional intelligence creates a relatable story. Are there any other skills I should be aware of?

Coach Ram: Authenticity is the foundation of business storytelling. Being true to yourself makes your story credible and fosters trust among your audience.

Piyush: Is there anything else I should keep in mind?

Coach Ram: Adaptability is key, Piyush. Business storytelling is not a one-size-fits-all approach. You need to be adaptable and adjust your storytelling based on the audience and context. This ensures that your story resonates with diverse listeners, whether it is one-one, communicating with a manager, communicating with peers, or communicating with superiors. Each situation demands a different response.

Piyush: Thank you for all these insights.

Piyush presented his story to his colleagues. There were facts and figures about his professional wins. Most importantly, the challenges he faced and how he rose through them. With that, he'd turned his imposter syndrome into a narrative of resilience.

Colleague: Piyush, inspiring presentation. I had no idea you went through so much. It makes your effort even more commendable.

The battle against imposter syndrome wasn't linear for Piyush. When there were moments of self-doubt, he engaged in self-compassion.

Piyush *(reflecting)*: It's okay to feel doubt, but I won't let it define me. I've worked hard, learned from my experiences, and I deserve my success.

Piyush understood that imposter syndrome might linger at the edges, but it no longer held the reins of his worthiness. His newfound belief in his abilities pushed him forward.

The battle against imposter syndrome is not fought with grand gestures but with the daily practice of acknowledging one's worth.

Self-Coaching Questions

Imposter Syndrome Reflection:

- What specific situations trigger feelings of imposter syndrome for you?
- Can you identify beliefs that stop you from talking about your achievements?
- Have you considered incorporating mindfulness practices to become more aware of negative self-talk?

Business Storytelling:

- How would you describe your current clarity and conciseness in conveying messages?

Journaling Success:

- Are you currently journaling your successes, both big, small, and anything in-between?
- Do you use your past successes to motivate yourself during challenging times? Why or why not?
- In what ways can journaling contribute to your goal-setting process for the future?

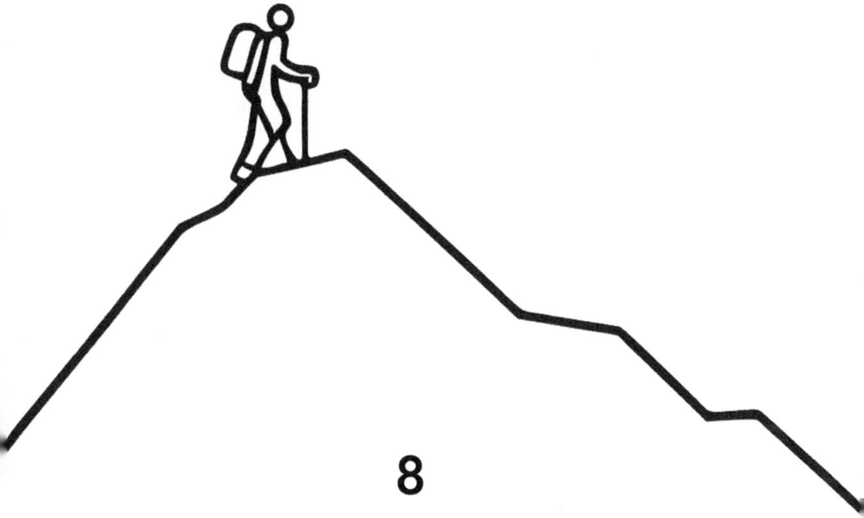

8

Dealing with Dilemmas

Gain clarity into your values and vision

In our work lives, dilemmas appear like mysterious forks in the road, forcing us to think about ourselves.

Self-Reflective Questionnaire

As we get ready to dive into the maze associated with career decisions, let's shed light on the hidden corners of self-awareness with some honest responses:

Current Dilemma Strategy:

- Reflect on past dilemmas: In the past, what have been my typical responses to career dilemmas? Have I leaned more towards caution or bold, decisive action?
- Emotional quotient: Am I in touch with my emotions when faced with dilemmas? Do emotions guide my decisions, or do I maintain an analytical stance?

Clarity of Career Vision:

- Defining success: What does success look like for me? What educational qualifications, work experiences, or job titles do I want to acquire in 5, 10, or 15 years?

- Alignment with values: Does my current career align with my values and long-term aspirations? Are there aspects that require realignment?

Balancing Short-Term and Long-Term Goals:

- Immediate vs. future impact: When faced with a dilemma, do I prioritize short-term gains or consider the potential long-term consequences of my decisions?
- Alignment with purpose: To what extent do my career choices align with my overarching life purpose?

Role of Intuition:

- Trusting intuition: Do I trust my intuition when making career decisions? Can I recall instances where following my instincts led to positive outcomes?

This reflective journey helps us face the dilemmas that punctuate our professional lives.

As Piyush grew his network, he noticed many individuals dealt with career dilemmas. He met Coach Ram to share his findings.

Piyush: Coach Ram, people seem to be at a crossroads in their careers. They don't know how to get their next promotion, follow their passion, and find work-life balance.

Coach Ram: You're right, Piyush. The modern professional landscape is filled with choices and uncertainties. Individuals feel torn between different paths.

Piyush: Take the dilemma of pursuing a stable job versus following your passion. Many people struggle with this decision; weighing the security of a paycheck against the desire for fulfillment.

Coach Ram: Yes, a classic dilemma! People often grapple with the fear of financial instability if they pursue their passion, but at the same time, they yearn for a sense of purpose in their work.

Piyush: And then there's the choice between advancing into leadership roles or specializing in a particular field.

Coach Ram: Exactly, Piyush. Some individuals face the dilemma of whether to broaden their skill set by taking on leadership positions or to deepen their expertise in a specific area. This decision requires careful consideration of our long-term career goals.

Piyush: Work-life balance is another big one. Many of my colleagues struggle to balance their professional responsibilities and personal lives. They're constantly juggling competing priorities.

Coach Ram: Achieving work-life balance is a challenge in today's fast-paced world. It requires setting boundaries, prioritizing tasks, and making time for self-care amid work pressure.

Piyush: And what about the dilemma of entrepreneurship versus sticking with a stable job? It seems like more and more people are drawn to starting their own business, but they're hesitant to take the leap.

Coach Ram: Starting a business involves risks and uncertainties. It requires planning, assessing risks, and embracing uncertainty. Many professionals fear failure. So, they choose the stability of a traditional job.

Piyush: Lastly, there's the dilemma of furthering education versus gaining work experience. Many people debate whether to pursue advanced degrees or gain hands-on experience.

Coach Ram: Continuing education opens doors to new opportunities but gaining practical experience is also invaluable. Individuals should assess their career goals and choose a path that aligns with their aspirations and values.

Piyush: You know, Coach, I wonder why we face these dilemmas in the first place. There's this inner conflict between what we think we should do and what we truly want.

Coach Ram: These dilemmas stem from societal expectations, personal values, and a desire for fulfillment.

Reflect on your priorities, aspirations, and values to make informed career decisions.

Piyush: So, we need to understand ourselves and our values instead of following others.

Coach Ram: Absolutely, Piyush. Self-awareness is key to navigating these dilemmas. When we have clarity about our values, goals, and priorities, we make the right decisions.

Piyush: That's reassuring to hear. But, Coach, how do we overcome the fear of missing out (FOMO) and the urge to compare ourselves to others?

Coach Ram: It's normal to feel envious or inadequate when we see others succeed or pursue their passions. However, everyone's journey is unique, and comparisons only breed discontent.

Piyush: So, how can we find clarity amid the dilemmas and distractions?

Coach Ram: One word, Piyush—anchoring. By anchoring ourselves to our career vision, values, and goals, we create a foundation that helps us stay grounded despite the chaos. When we know and trust where we're headed and what matters to us, the noise of comparison and FOMO fades away.

Piyush: It's like having a guiding light that keeps us focused on our path, even when the journey gets challenging.

Coach Ram: Exactly.

Piyush: Coach Ram, having self-awareness and a clear career vision is great. But it's hard to know where to start. How do I develop self-awareness?

Coach Ram: Well, self-awareness is a journey. It involves reflection and seeking guidance. One way to start is by journaling regularly. Writing your thoughts, feelings, and aspirations shows what matters to you.

Coach Ram: Engage in conversations with your mentors and coaches as and when you can. Reflect on their insights and your assumptions.

Piyush: My friend Vedant is an ethical hacker. He has received an offer for a leadership role. He also has an acceptance letter from a foreign university to study cybersecurity. He can't decide which opportunity to pursue.

Coach Ram acknowledged the weight of the decision.

Coach Ram: Let's delve into what each choice means for Vedant. What draws him to the leadership role, and what sparks his interest in further studies?

Piyush's friend, Aisha, knocked on the partly open door. Aisha is a banker, but is keen on pursuing research and then getting into academics. She wanted to share her own academic dilemma.

Aisha: Sorry to interrupt your meeting but I'm at a similar crossroads. I want to continue my studies, but I'm worried about how I can support myself financially while studying.

Coach Ram welcomed Aisha, acknowledging the complexity of career decisions.

Coach Ram: Aisha, Piyush's another friend is contemplating between leadership and specialization. What about you? What's the driving force for further studies and what financial concerns are holding you back?

Aisha conveyed her passion for research. Financial constraints, however, loomed as a formidable barrier to the pursuit of her intellectual curiosity. She cannot afford to take sabbatical for studies at this point.

Coach Ram and Piyush deliberated.

Piyush: Aisha, have you considered financial aid or part-time work while studying? These options alleviate the financial burden.

Aisha: I hadn't thought about part-time work. Coach Ram, what do you think about balancing work and study?

Coach Ram: It requires planning and assessing your capacity. Piyush, what are your thoughts?

The trio exchanged ideas, concerns, and solutions. Coach Ram provided actionable insights.

Through dialogue, Piyush and Aisha witnessed the power of collaborative problem-solving.

Coach Ram: Piyush, Aisha, these dilemmas are opportunities for growth. Let's create a toolkit tailored to your situations. Piyush, envision Vedant's leadership role; Aisha, consider financial support during your studies. Together, we'll navigate these crossroads.

Coach Ram guided Piyush and Aisha. He outlined the steps, the obstacles and the solution for these obstacles.

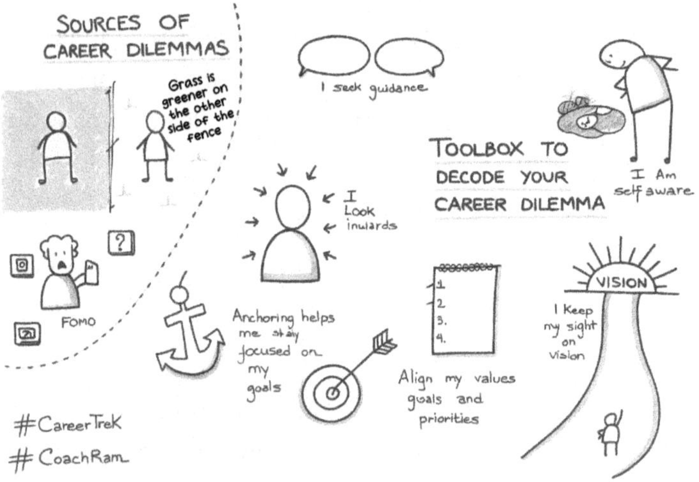

Self-Coaching Questions

Clarifying Core Values:

- What are my values at work?
- Does my current career align with these values?
- Are there aspects of my professional life that seem incongruent with what I hold dear?

Enhancing Career Vision:

- What are my short-term and long-term goals that align with this vision?

Leveraging Mentorship and Coaching:

- Have I actively sought the guidance of mentors or coaches in the past?
- What are the challenges or dilemmas I need help sorting through?

Balancing Passion and Pragmatism:

- How do I currently balance pursuing my passions with meeting financial or stability needs?
- Are there adjustments I can make to align passion and pragmatism in my career choices?
- What sacrifices am I willing to make, and what boundaries do I need to set in this balance?

Building a Support System:

- Who comprises my support system, both personally and professionally? Who cheers me up when I lose motivation after stressful days at work? Who gives me guidance on my next professional move?

- Do I communicate my career dilemmas and seek support from this network regularly?

Setting Realistic Expectations:

- What milestones do I want to achieve at work and how soon do I want them?
- Are these expectations realistic, or do they contribute to stress?

In the quest to make career choices, dilemmas are inevitable. Armed with self-awareness, a clear career vision, and the wisdom gained through conversations with mentors and coaches, you can face the most complex dilemmas. Embrace the challenges. Find your strength.

9

Manufacturing Your Luck

Discover the secret of making your own luck

Some people seem to have all the luck, and some just don't seem to get a break. Is luck just a matter of rolling the dice, or can we steer our ships toward luck? Join me as I solve this puzzle and explore how chances and choices affect our lives. There are some things we can't change, like the weather but luck isn't one of them. There is a sneaky way to make your luck.

Let's look for the secret tools to manipulate luck. Let's use serendipity's chaos to sprinkle lucky dust on our confusion. Let's get the rabbit's foot ready and roll the dice of fate together!

We either ignore the chances and call it destiny or embrace the chances and call it luck.

Self-Reflective Questionnaire

Before we look at how luck is made, let's pause to introspect. Engage with these questions to understand your perspective:

1. Do I consider myself lucky?
    - Reflect not just on external circumstances but on your internal beliefs. Consider instances where you felt lucky or unlucky and

analyze the narratives associated with these experiences.

2. What is my self-talk when it comes to luck and opportunities?
   - Delve into the dialogues that unfold within your mind. Are you prone to self-limiting beliefs, or do you embrace opportunities with optimism?
3. How open-minded am I to possibilities? Do I seize opportunities when they arise?
   - Assess your receptivity to unforeseen possibilities. Reflect on past instances where unexpected opportunities presented themselves. Did you seize those moments, or did hesitation and overthinking prevail?
4. Am I aware of the role of privilege or disadvantage in my life?
   - Consider the socio-economic and cultural context of your background. Acknowledge privileges or challenges that may influence your journey. Awareness of these factors is crucial in understanding the nuances of your relationship with luck.
5. Do I believe in making my luck; and choosing actions to influence my fortune, or do I attribute my success and failure to external forces?

One day, Coach Ram invited a few of his friends and colleagues for lunch, which later turned into a discussion over luck.

Vivek: You know, guys, luck seems like such a fickle thing, doesn't it? Some people seem to have it fall into their laps, while others are left scratching their heads wondering when their turn will come.

Coach Ram: Absolutely, Vivek. Luck has a way of playing favorites sometimes. But let me tell you, there's more to it than meets the eye.

Piyush: Really? I've always thought luck was about being in the right place at the right time.

Coach Ram: Well, Piyush, luck isn't just about chance; it's about being prepared to make the most of those opportunities when they come knocking.

Vivek: That's right! It's like having your fishing rod ready when the big one bites. You must be prepared to reel it in!

Piyush: So, what can we do to increase our luck quotient?

Coach Ram: That's where the concept of manufacturing luck comes into play. It's about creating opportunities rather than waiting for them to fall into our laps.

Vivek: Exactly! And one of the keys to manufacturing luck is using "serendipity hooks."

Piyush: Serendipity hooks? What are those?

Vivek: They're conversation starters on steroids. Instead of just talking about what we do, we share our passions, our interests—basically, anything that could spark a connection.

Coach Ram: Yes. When we are asked to introduce ourselves professionally, we usually tend to talk about our current role or facts about our career. Talking about our interests and plans paves way for serendipity hooks. And you never know when those connections might lead to something amazing. It's all about being open to new possibilities.

Vivek: Luck is what happens when preparation meets opportunity.

Coach Ram: And with passion, persistence, being in the right place, and doing the right things, we can stack the odds of luck in our favor.

Piyush: Well, I'm feeling luckier already! Thanks for shedding some light on this, guys.

Vivek: Anytime, Piyush. And remember, luck may not always be on our side but with the right mindset, we can make our luck!

Piyush: Wait a minute, what about the three P's you mentioned earlier, Coach Ram? You know, Passion, Persistence, and Placement?

Coach Ram: Ah yes, the three P's! They're the components of manufacturing luck.

Vivek: They are the secret ingredients of cooking up success!

Coach Ram: Indeed, Vivek. Passion fuels the fire. It keeps us motivated even when our situations get tough. It drives us to keep pushing forward, no matter the obstacles. The quote that comes to my mind is, "Success is going from one failed attempt to another failed attempt without loss of enthusiasm."

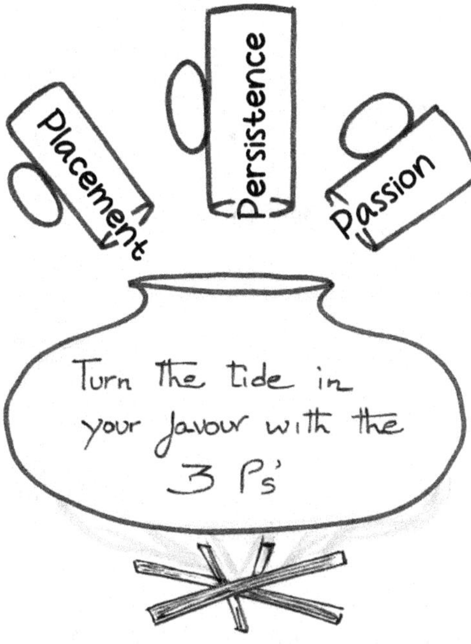

Piyush: And what about Persistence?

Coach Ram: Persistence is the glue that holds it all together. It's the determination to keep going, even when we face setbacks or challenges. Without persistence, passion can fizzle out, but with it, we can weather any storm.

Vivek: And Placement?

Coach Ram: Placement is all about positioning ourselves for success. It's about being in the right place at the right time, networking with the right people, staying up-to-date on industry trends, and being ready to seize opportunities.

Vivek: Luck isn't something that happens to us; it's something we create for ourselves.

Coach Ram: With the three P's in our toolkit, we can manufacture luck and pave the way for our success. There are eight rules or ways to create luck. These ways offer insights into how luck works and how we can influence it.

Coach Ram leaned back in his chair, his eyes twinkling with excitement, and asked: Have you ever heard of the serendipity mindset?

Piyush furrowed his brow, intrigued. "Serendipity mindset? Isn't that just about luck?"

Coach Ram: It's more than luck, Piyush. It's about creating opportunities for luck to find you. Let me tell you about the eight rules Karla Starr shared in the book, *Can You Learn to Be Lucky*?

Piyush: What are these rules?

Coach Ram: First, sociability is a predictor of opportunity. The more you network and connect with others, the more chances you have for serendipitous encounters.

Piyush: So, it's about who you know?

Coach Ram: Exactly. And that brings us to rule number two: proximity. The closer you are to someone, the more likely they are to care for you and help you.

Piyush: Interesting. So, it's not only about making connections but also nurturing them.

Coach Ram: It is the quality of your engagement and the mindspace you can create. And appearances matter, too. Rule number three: dress for success. When you look the part, people are more likely to trust and respect you. Your effort to look presentable demonstrates professionalism.

Piyush: Confidence plays a role, too, doesn't it?

Coach Ram: Absolutely. Confidence is the fourth way to create luck. When you believe in yourself, others are more likely to believe in you, too. It is good to reflect if you take bets on yourself. Many times, we tend to undermine ourselves and deny ourselves opportunities.

Coach Ram: Another way to get lucky is by having access to resources. Being able to access people, platforms, and finances can open doors you never knew existed.

Engaging with people without agenda periodically is key for this to transpire. No agenda conversations build real bonds with people, and eventually, something good will turn out.

Piyush: Right. What else, Coach?

Coach Ram: Rule number six is about self-discipline. The more disciplined you are, the more opportunities you'll attract.

Piyush smiled, connecting the dots to guess the next rule, "And staying curious. That's important, too, right?"

"Spot on," Coach Ram said with a grin. "Rule number seven: stay curious. The more curious you are, the more likely you are to stumble upon unexpected opportunities. Having an experimental attitude is more likely to open new opportunities."

Piyush nodded enthusiastically, "This makes sense, Coach. What's the final rule?"

"Rule number eight. Going last can improve your success rate. Sometimes, it pays to be patient and wait for the right moment to shine. Being the last one to speak, being the one to be interviewed, and being the last one to make your move empowers you and the other party with more perspective. Research proves that we are harsh judges at the beginning and become less critical towards the end," explained Coach Ram.

Piyush felt inspired. "Thanks, Coach. I'll keep these rules in mind as I navigate my career."

"You're welcome, Piyush. Remember, luck is more predictable than you think. With the right mindset and actions, you can create your luck."

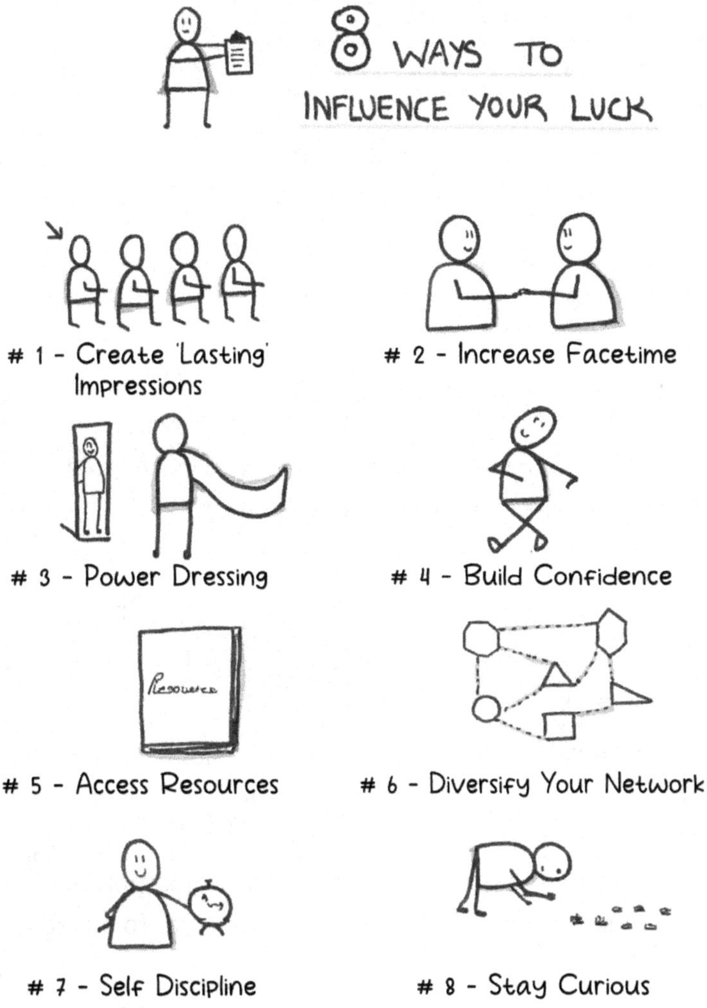
8 WAYS TO
INFLUENCE YOUR LUCK
1 - Create 'Lasting' Impressions
2 - Increase Facetime
3 - Power Dressing
4 - Build Confidence
Resources
5 - Access Resources
6 - Diversify Your Network
7 - Self Discipline
8 - Stay Curious

Coach Ram gave Piyush some questions to ponder which are as follows:

Self-Coaching Questions

Reflecting on Beliefs:

- How do I define luck, and do I believe I can control it?
- Can I identify limiting beliefs that make me think luck is out of my reach?

Approach to Possibilities:

- What opportunities have I had recently in my professional and personal life? What was my attitude toward these opportunities? Was I open to exploration, or did I shut them down?
- How can I reframe my limiting beliefs to accept unexpected opportunities?

Flexibility in Goals:

- What are my goals for my professional life? Do I feel comfortable adjusting them to explore other possibilities?

Enhancing Introductions:

- How do I introduce myself to new people at work?
- Am I willing to talk about incorporating serendipity hooks in my introductions to create a bond with my connections?

- What are some ways I can talk about my ambitions and struggles to seem relatable without getting into details?

Strategic Placement:

- How can I enhance my networking efforts to increase my visibility and access to potential opportunities?

Mindset Shift:

- Do I believe that luck is a collaboration between chance and preparedness?
- In what areas of my life can I actively work on shifting my mindset from waiting for luck to intentionally manufacturing it?

These self-coaching questions are designed to make you see that luck can be made. The message is clear: luck is not a happenstance event; it is a deliberate creation. It is the amalgamation of our openness to possibilities and readiness to act on them. When we create our own luck, we take charge of our story and turn every moment into a chance to shape our future Don't wait for luck. Make your own. Be the architect of your fate.

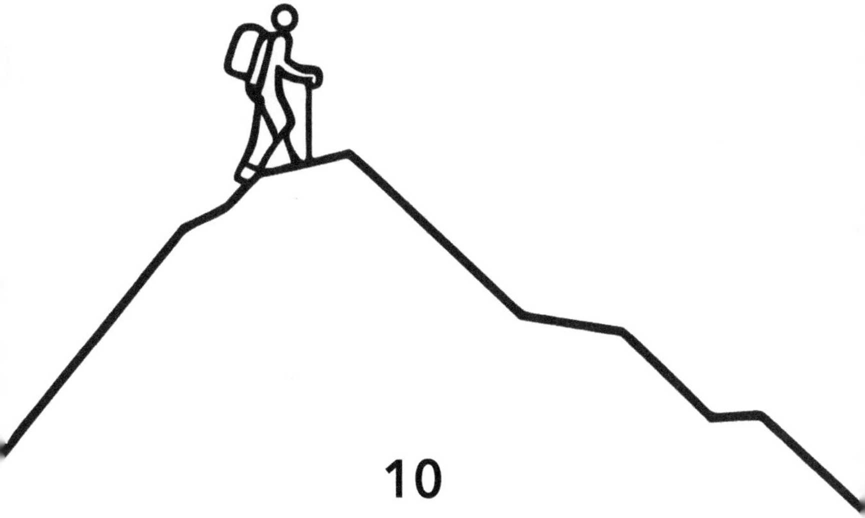

10

Individual Development Plans (IDPs)

The roadmap to chart your career destiny

Our careers do not look the same. So, too, our challenges. There is no one-size-fits-all solution to fix our unique problems. How we want our careers to develop depends on how we plan. Without a plan, it's like going on a trek without an itinerary and map—directionless, uncertain, and prone to wandering. An Individual Development Plan or IDP offers purpose, direction, and a step-by-step approach to achieving your professional goals.

IDP is a personalized blueprint that you can use to set your developmental goals; improve your skills and achieve your milestones. It serves as a reference point, ensuring that every professional step aligns with your vision.

While job-specific skills guarantee immediate success in a particular role, they often fall short of providing long-term career growth. Long-term growth needs development of leadership skills and domain skills.

You might wonder why a list of skills suited to a job might not be enough in today's fast-paced work market. Because businesses evolve, you need to be able to adapt and think ahead. In these situations, IDPs give you a structured way to find and build skills that are useful in your current job and will also help with future opportunities and challenges.

Self-Reflective Questionnaire

Before we understand IDPs, let's reflect:

1. Have you made an IDP for yourself? How frequently do you review it?
2. Is your IDP focused on short-term job needs or long-term career goals?
3. Is your IDP aligned with your personal board of directors?

One day, Piyush's mentee reached out to him to seek clarity about his career. Piyush needed to consult with Coach Ram to use the right approach to guide his mentee.

Coach Ram: So, Piyush, let's delve into this whole career navigation thing. You know, skills have a shorter shelf life these days.

Piyush: Yeah, it's like what you mentioned earlier about how someone's skills in Photoshop might lose their value with new technology.

Coach Ram: Exactly! And that's why it's crucial to have a plan for your career, not just your job. Your job might stay the same, but your career is the bigger picture.

Piyush: So, how do you navigate your career path in a way that benefits you?

Coach Ram: Well, there are different approaches. You've got the bullseye approach, which is all about hitting a specific target, like getting a particular job title. For a career, the compass approach is better. The compass approach is having a career vision and taking toward it, without focusing on a niche path.

Piyush: The compass approach allows for more exploration and learning, right?

Coach Ram: Exactly! It's not as sharp as the bullseye, but it gives you direction and flexibility. With the compass approach, you're open to uncertainty and new possibilities. Remember the serendipity hooks from the last chapter, you allow luck to do its magic with this approach.

The Bullseye Approach is like aiming at a specific job title or role, say, *"I want to be a Product Manager at Google by 2026."*

You focus all your energy on hitting that exact target: gaining the right degree, building the exact skills, and applying only to that kind of role.

✅ It's precise, but rigid. If the target moves or disappears (say, the role changes or the company shifts focus), you're stuck.

The Compass Approach, on the other hand, is like saying, *"I want to build a meaningful career in tech that involves solving user problems through product thinking."*

You have a direction, not a fixed destination. You might explore roles in UX, data, product, or even startups along the way.

✅ It gives you **direction** and **freedom to adapt**, especially in a world where skills and jobs keep evolving.

Example to Bring It to Life:
Imagine someone who learns Photoshop and says, "I want to be a Senior Designer at XYZ Agency by 2025."

→ That's **bullseye**. But what if Photoshop becomes obsolete? That goal collapses.

Now, imagine someone who says, "I want to work at the intersection of creativity and tech."

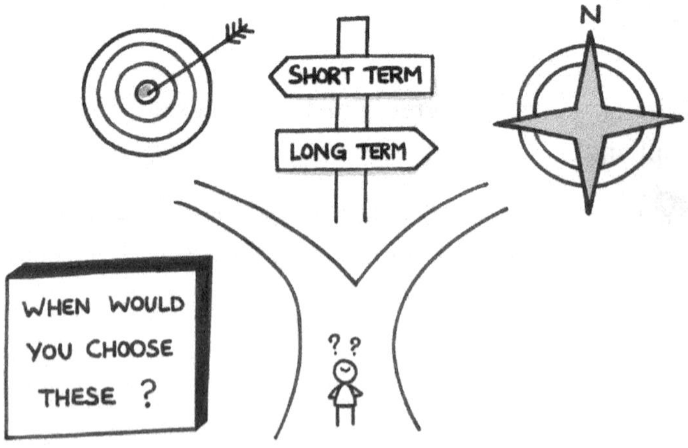

→ That's **compass**. They may start with design, later explore motion graphics, UX, or even AI art tools—and still be aligned with their vision.

Piyush: That sounds like a dynamic way to look at your career.

Coach Ram: It sure is! And to make the most of the compass approach, you need a structured development plan. You need to map out your aspirations, set goals, and take ownership of your career path.

Piyush: So, it's about having a plan that adapts to changes along the way?

Coach Ram: Absolutely, Piyush. Think of an Individual Development Plan (IDP) as your compass in the professional world. Let me elaborate on this with a story. There's this remarkable professional, Sarah, who works in film production. Now, Sarah is fantastic at her current job. But she realized that to reach a leadership position, she needed more than just excellence. That's where the IDP came into play.

Piyush: How did an IDP help Sarah?

Coach Ram: Well, let me break it down. Sarah paused to decide where she wanted to take her career. She envisioned herself leading productions and making strategic decisions. An IDP is a roadmap for such aspirations.

Piyush: But how does it work? What's in this roadmap?

Coach Ram: Good question, Piyush. The IDP starts with a thorough self-assessment. Sarah looked at her strengths, weaknesses, and where she saw herself in the future. Then, she identified the skills and experiences needed to bridge the gap between her current state and career goals.

Piyush: So, it's about setting goals?

Coach Ram: First, Sarah identified her long-term career goals. She wanted to move from an expert in her current role to a leader who makes decisions.

Piyush: Like a career vision!

Coach Ram: Yes! Then, she looked at her current skills and what she needed for her future role. This gap analysis helped her pinpoint the areas she needed to work on.

Piyush: So, then it's about self-awareness.

Coach Ram: Spot on, Piyush! Self-awareness is the foundation. Now, to fill those skill gaps, Sarah set SMART goals.

SMART Goals are a simple way to set clear and achievable goals. The word **SMART** stands for:

- **S**pecific: Be clear about *what* you want to achieve.
  For eg.: *"I want to improve my presentation skills."*
- **M**easurable: Know *how* you'll track progress.
  For eg.: *"I'll deliver three presentations in the next month."*

- **A**chievable: Make sure the goal is realistic.
  For eg.: *"I'll practice twice a week and get feedback."*
- **R**elevant: The goal should matter to your overall growth.
  For eg.: *"This will help me lead client meetings better."*
- **T**ime-bound: Set a deadline.
  For eg.: *"I'll achieve this by the end of next month."*

Piyush: That sounds practical.

Coach Ram: It is. And here's the bonus. An IDP is not a one-time thing. It's a living document. Sarah regularly reviewed her progress, adjusted her goals if needed, and celebrated achievements along the way.

Piyush: So, is it about being adaptable?

Coach Ram: Absolutely! Careers are dynamic, and an effective IDP adapts to changes. Now, the three E approach—Education, Experience, and Exposure—played a crucial role in Sarah's plan.

Piyush: Could you get into the details?

Coach Ram: Let me break it down. Building competency requires a multi-pronged approach of 3E's. 3E is also referred to as "70:20:10".

The 3E Development Model is a simple framework to help people grow in their careers. It includes:

1. **Experience**: Learning by doing. You grow by taking on new tasks, projects, or roles.

2. **Exposure**: Learning from others. This includes mentoring, coaching, networking, or watching how others work.
3. **Education**: Learning through formal methods like courses, workshops, or reading.

Think of it like this:
You **do** (Experience).
You **see and learn from others** (Exposure).
You **study** (Education).
All three together help build skills and capabilities.

Let's dive into examples for each of the three Es in Sarah's approach. Starting with the first E (Education-10%), Sarah signed up for a nine-month leadership development program with a renowned B-school. The cohort had professionals from many organizations with similar aspirations and expectations from the program. The program lay a strong scientific foundation for leadership concepts. It also gave her perspective and widened her opportunities.

Piyush: That's the first E.

Coach Ram: Right! The second E is Experience. Sarah looked for projects and tasks that were outside of her present job. She volunteered to lead a cross-functional team for the launch of a new web series. She took on a project requiring her to work with people from different departments. By performing many roles and their responsibilities, Sarah diversified her skills and showed that she could handle challenging problems. Additionally, she volunteered to support her mentor (PBOD) on a project as well.

Piyush: And the third?

Coach Ram: Exposure makes up 20% of competency. Sarah exposed herself to opportunities. She attended immersion sessions, conferences, and networking events. She also signed up for sessions with coaches and mentors to support her skill development. She volunteered for strategic initiatives, task forces, or working groups, giving herself chances to meet production heads and learn about different points of view within the company.

Piyush: So, it's not just about skills but also about gaining new perspectives.

Coach Ram: Exactly! An effective IDP doesn't only focus on technical skills. It helps you become a well-rounded professional with a thorough understanding of the business.

Piyush: So, combining these three Es helped Sarah grow. Doing all this requires someone to step out of their comfort zone right?

Coach Ram: Yes, Piyush, I would call it courage. Beyond the IDP, for success as a professional one needs three forms of courage; TRY courage, TRUST courage, and

COURAGE TO CONQUER MY CAREER
I will take a bet on me.
I will trust and Let go of control.
#coachram
I will speak up.
#careertrek

TELL courage. Bill Treasurer talks about these in his book, *Courage Goes To Work*.

Piyush: Can you explain the three ways to exercise courage?

Coach Ram: Sure. The first type, TRY courage, is about making the first attempt at something new, even if it's daunting. It's the courage to take that first step.

Piyush: Like when Sarah took on new projects outside her comfort zone?

Coach Ram: Exactly. The second type, TRUST courage, involves letting go of our need to control everything and having faith in others. You need it while working in teams and delegating tasks.

It's about trusting the process, even when it's not in your control. The third type, TELL courage, is about voicing your opinion, even if it means you might be seen as a maverick or an outsider.

Piyush: That sounds tough. Speaking up can be risky.

Coach Ram: It is, but it's vital. Many people stay quiet to avoid rocking the boat, but progress often comes from honest conversations.

Piyush: Got that. I feel equipped to embark on my IDP.

Coach Ram: Absolutely, Piyush. Just like you wouldn't embark on a journey without a map, your career trek becomes easier to navigate with an IDP. It's your compass in the professional world, guiding you toward your true north.

Piyush: I can see how valuable that can be. Thanks for sharing, Coach!

Coach Ram: My pleasure, Piyush. Remember, the journey is as important as the destination. An IDP ensures you enjoy the ride while staying focused on where you want to go. Also, to figure out areas where you can improve, ask for feedback from people who work with you. This feedback can be anonymous, meaning they don't have to put their name on it. It's called "360-degree feedback" because you' get input from all directions—your peers, your manager, and even yourself. This way, you can see what others think about your strengths and weaknesses, helping you identify areas for development.

To conclude, the shelf life of skills is constantly getting shorter, so it's crucial to learn and upskill. Even if your job doesn't change, the way you do a job keeps changing with the advent of new technologies and market trends.

What's the difference between a job and a career? Well, a job focuses on short-term needs. It is driven by your manager or the project you are working on. On the other hand, a career is your journey to reaching your potential. It's a series of jobs that align with your goals and abilities. A career is long-term. While many companies offer jobs, only a few help you build a career. But remember, the responsibility for shaping your career lies with you. You can seek guidance and support from your manager or organization, but ultimately, it's up to you to take charge. You need self-awareness and proactive planning to get ahead.

As we carry out our daily tasks, let's focus on our growth and plan our careers intentionally. The best way to predict the future is to create it, and your Individual Development Plan is your ticket to realizing your aspirations.

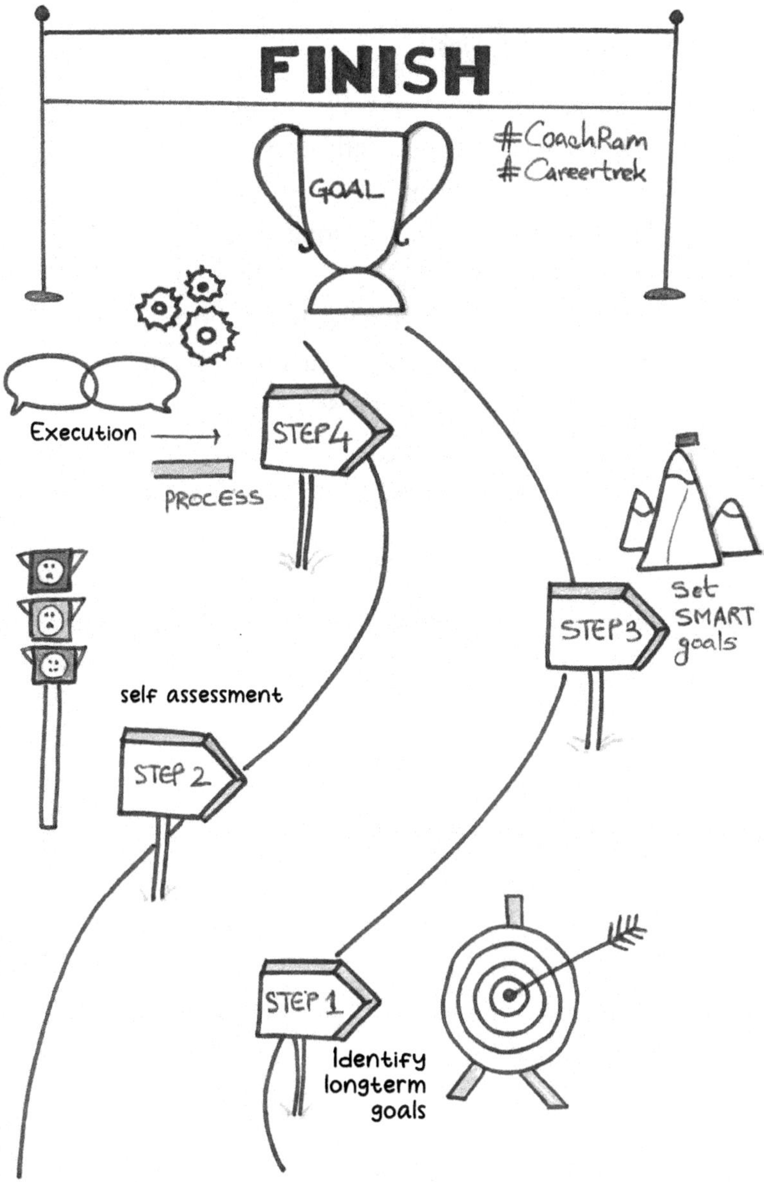
FINISH
GOAL
#CoachRam
#Careertrek
Execution
PROCESS
STEP 4
Set SMART goals
STEP 3
self assessment
STEP 2
STEP 1
Identify longterm goals

Self-Coaching Questions

- What is your vision for your career?
- What skills do you currently possess that set you apart from your peers?
- In what ways do your existing skills align with your career goals?
- Have you identified professionals whose career paths you admire, and what insights can you gain from their experiences?

11

Building a Personal Brand

The 101 of your personal brand

Your personal brand is who you are beyond your job title or the firm you work at. It serves as your professional identification, reputation, and calling card. Whether you are aware of it or not, you already have a personal brand. A personal brand isn't only designed to get you jobs. A strong personal brand helps you attract opportunities beyond jobs (remember serendipity hooks). It contains your ideals, competence, and what distinguishes you from others.

Building your personal brand entails sharing your skills and thoughts with others. You can accomplish this through a variety of channels, including blogging on platforms such as LinkedIn, Quora, or Medium; hosting podcasts or live shows; joining and contributing to communities related to your field; maintaining a presence on social media platforms such as Instagram, X, or Facebook; and attending industry forums such as conferences, round tables, and networking events. Your performance in the current role and organization influences your personal brand. Your personal brand is what people remember about you in your absence. Your personal brand is what makes you get into the go-to list of who matters. It is the x-factor that differentiates you from the crowd.

Many people feel overwhelmed and unsure about how to build their personal brand. Start somewhere modestly, focusing on what is comfortable for you. Could be a simple LinkedIn post, a small guest lecture and anything beyond. It is natural to experience hurdles and setbacks. The key is to remain committed and go forward. With time and dedication, you'll discover your groove and build a strong personal brand that reflects who you are and your thought leadership.

Self-Reflective Questionnaire

1. Do you believe you should be intentional (planned/strategic) about your personal brand?
2. What is your personal brand?
3. Are there any misconceptions you hold about personal branding that might be limiting your growth?
4. What are my strengths and skills that set me apart from others in my field? What digital platforms and offline events such as internal meetings can I use to showcase my story?

Building a personal brand is about creating a distinct identity that goes beyond your job title. It's about presenting who you are, your values, and your contributions to the ecosystem.

Piyush brought his curiosity about branding to Coach Ram. Coach Ram began a story about Ananya, a counselling psychologist and one of his coaches, who experienced the impact of personal branding in her career.

Coach Ram: Piyush, personal branding is like the story you tell the professional world about yourself. Let me share a real-life example to illustrate its power. Ananya, a counselling psychologist, discovered the influence of personal branding in a rather unexpected way.

Piyush: How do we tell our story in the professional world?

Coach Ram: Absolutely, Piyush. Now, imagine Ananya who is passionate about helping her clients with their mental health issues. She has to find solutions for their problems. Instead of keeping that knowledge to herself, she shared her insights and experiences in articles. Those articles became her professional story, showcasing her expertise in psychological counselling.

Piyush: So, writing articles is personal branding?

Coach Ram: No. However, there's much more to personal branding than just this. Let me get to that later. So, Ananya's articles were like chapters of her professional journey. They were authentic, reflected her insights, and experiences with her clients. They were valuable to others in her field. It's not just about doing your job; it's about sharing your unique perspective and knowledge.

Piyush: But how does this impact her career?

Coach Ram: That's the interesting part. As Ananya's articles gained attention, people in her industry began noticing her. Her name became associated with insightful content. Her high self-confidence, opened doors to opportunities beyond her current role. She received invitations to mental health awareness campaigns and panel discussions. Renowned psychologists recognized her at these appearances.

Piyush: So, personal branding is like creating a reputation for yourself?

Coach Ram: Exactly, Piyush. You want to be known for your expertise. All things being equal between two people, the one with a stronger personal brand has the edge. Ananya's articles weren't just about showcasing what she knew; they were about positioning herself as someone who adds value to the industry.

Piyush: But isn't personal branding for influencers or celebrities?

Coach Ram: That's a misconception, Piyush. Personal branding is for everyone. You're not chasing fame. You want to be recognized and respected by professionals in your field. This way you can eliminate competition.

Piyush: How do I get started with personal branding?

Coach Ram: Good question. Personal branding starts with understanding what you're passionate about and what unique perspective or knowledge you can share. You could write just like Ananya. You could also communicate through conferences, LinkedIn, team meetings, or content creation on YouTube or Instagram.

Piyush: So, we need to gain visibility in our professions.

Coach Ram: Spot on, Piyush. Visibility is crucial. When people know what you stand for and the value you bring, it opens avenues for and recognition. It's like letting others see the best of what you have to offer.

Piyush: This makes sense, Coach. It's like telling your professional story in a way that others remember.

Coach Ram: Absolutely, Piyush. A well-crafted professional story becomes a powerful tool to advance your career. You let your work and your perspective speak for itself. Remember, personal branding is a journey, not a destination. Start small, be consistent, and let yourself shine through.

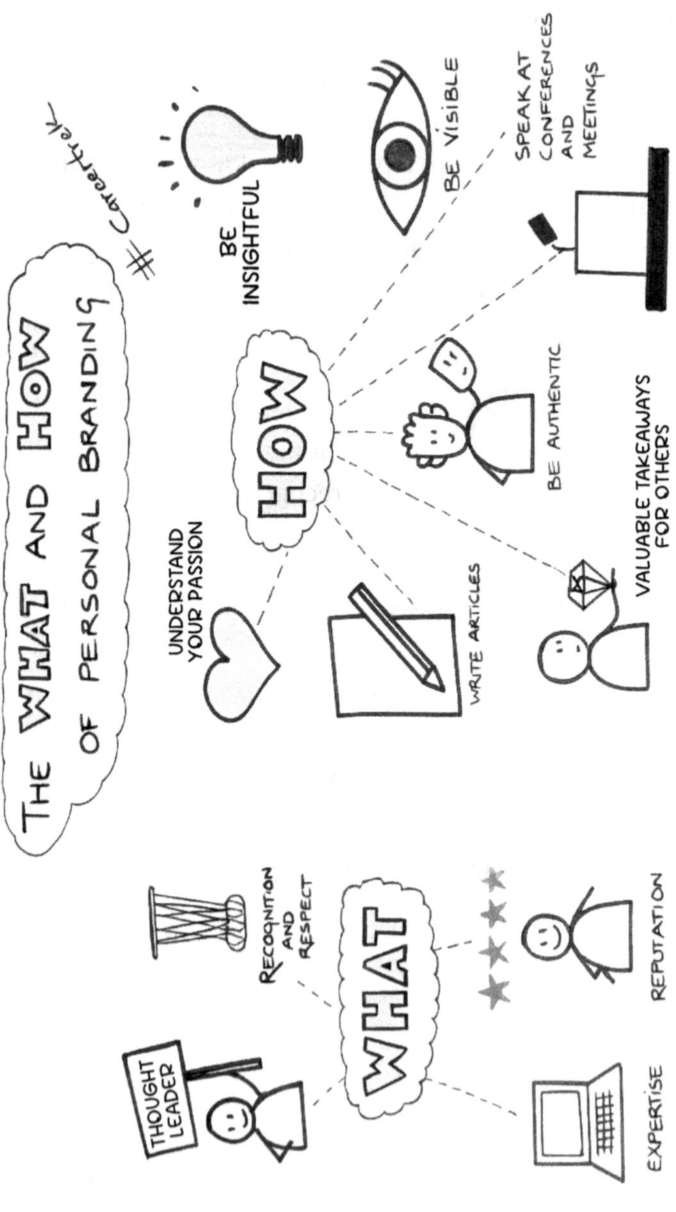
THE WHAT AND HOW OF PERSONAL BRANDING
#Careertrek
WHAT
THOUGHT LEADER
RECOGNITION AND RESPECT
REPUTATION
EXPERTISE
HOW
UNDERSTAND YOUR PASSION
WRITE ARTICLES
VALUABLE TAKEAWAYS FOR OTHERS
BE INSIGHTFUL
BE AUTHENTIC
BE VISIBLE
SPEAK AT CONFERENCES AND MEETINGS

Self-Coaching Questions

Defining Your Brand:

- What words or adjectives would you like people to use when describing you professionally?
- How would your colleagues, friends, or family currently describe your professional persona?
- What unique skills or talents do you possess that set you apart from others in your field?

Target Audience:

- Who is your target audience for your personal brand? (E.g., colleagues, industry peers, potential employers.)
- What aspects of your professional identity would resonate most with your target audience?

Online Presence:

- How do you currently present yourself on professional platforms like LinkedIn or other social media?
- Are there any improvements or updates you could make to enhance your online professional presence?
- What type of content (audio, video, short text, long articles, pictures, etc.) can you share online to reinforce your personal brand?

Learning and Growth:

- In what areas do you feel there is room for improvement in your professional skills or knowledge?
- How can your personal brand reflect a commitment to continuous learning and growth?
- Are there any upcoming industry trends or changes that you could incorporate into your brand narrative?

Feedback and Adaptation:

- How open are you to receiving feedback about your personal brand from colleagues or mentors?
- Are there regular checkpoints you can set to assess and refine your personal brand?

Overcoming Challenges:

- What challenges or obstacles do you foresee in building and promoting your personal brand?
- How can you overcome these challenges?
- Are there individuals with personal brands you admire? What lessons can you draw from their experiences?

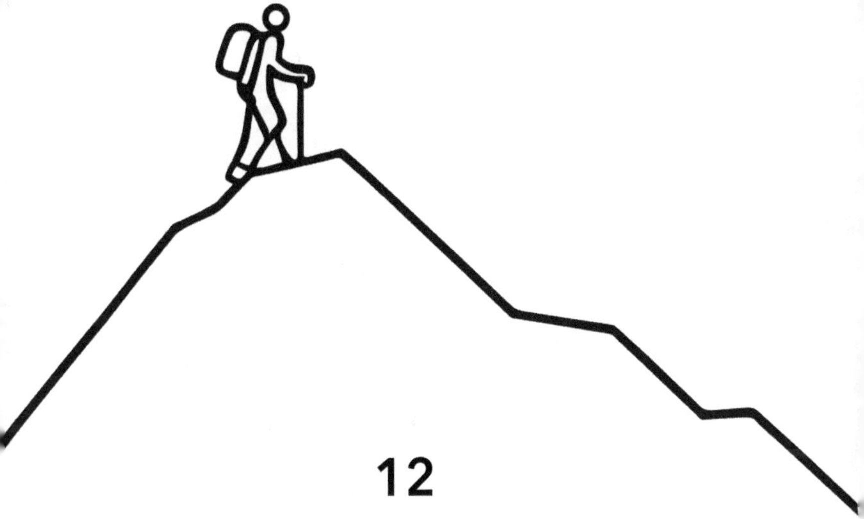

12

Managing Career Transitions

Beat your mid-career blues

The first half of your career often seems smooth sailing. Opportunities are abundant, and the path ahead appears wide open. However, as you progress into the second half, you encounter challenges. The road gets narrower, and the opportunities get fewer. In his book *Catalyst*, Chandramouli Venkatesan writes that most people thrive in the first half of their careers, while many struggle in the second half.

You may notice that the skills and attitude that brought success in the first half of your career don't yield the same results anymore. Welcome to the mid-career blues. You feel like you've reached a ceiling in your current role or specialization, and you question what comes next.

It's like standing at a crossroads, wondering whether to pursue a path towards general management roles or to pivot into a different area of expertise. To help gauge where you stand, you can do a self-reflection questionnaire to determine if you're experiencing a mid-career crisis.

Career growth is not just about the number of years you've been working but the diversity of experiences you've gained. Each experience adds depth and breadth to your professional journey, whether it's navigating through a team layoff or building a new team from scratch.

To avoid getting stuck in a rut or being pigeonholed into a certain role, diversify your work portfolio. This means seek new challenges and opportunities every few years, whether it's exploring a different industry, taking on a new role, or even relocating to a different city or country.

Self-Reflective Questionnaire

Answer these questions to discover if you are primed for a career transition (or) experiencing mid-career crisis:

- What fears or concerns do you associate with career transitions?

- Are you feeling stagnant in your current role or career path?
- Do you find yourself questioning your long-term career goals and aspirations?
- Are you experiencing a lack of motivation at work?
- Have you noticed a dip in your job satisfaction or happiness in your professional life?
- Are you feeling undervalued or underutilized in your current position?
- Do you find yourself longing for new challenges or opportunities to develop professionally?
- Are you feeling anxious about your future career prospects?
- Have you been contemplating a career change or transition?
- Do you feel like you've reached a plateau in your career progression, with limited opportunities for advancement?
- Are you experiencing conflicts between your personal values and the expectations of your current role or organization?

The misconception around career transitions is the idea of starting from scratch. View these transitions as a continuation of the professional journey, with each phase building upon the previous. Consider a book with different chapters—each career move is like turning a page, not closing the entire book. The skills, experiences, and lessons learned in one chapter carry forward, contributing to a layered narrative.

One of the key aspects of career transitions is to recognize transferable skills. These are skills acquired in one context but are highly applicable and valuable in another. They act as bridges, seamlessly connecting different roles and industries. For example, the analytical skills developed in a finance role might be transferable to a project management position. Another example to consider—let's say you manage projects in the IT sector. Your organizational and project management skills are highly transferable. These skills are valuable in roles beyond IT, such as operations or event management. Recognizing and leveraging these skills make career shifts fluid and less intimidating.

Coach Ram: Piyush, changing careers might seem daunting, but remember, it means evolving rather than starting anew. Imagine your career as a story. Each move is a new chapter. Your past experiences, skills, and lessons learned are like the plot twists that shape the narrative.

Piyush: I get that, Coach Ram, but how can someone accept a career transition without feeling like they're back at square one?

Coach Ram: The corporate world is full of myths that

can mislead you if you take them at face value. Let's bust some of those myths wide open. Ready?

Piyush: Absolutely. Let's get to it.

Coach Ram: Alright, here are some common career myths that we need to clear up:

> Myth 1: The organization is responsible for your career.

Piyush: I've always thought that if I work hard, my company will take care of my career progression.

Coach Ram: That's a common belief, but it's a myth. Your career is your responsibility. Organizations provide opportunities, but you need to manage your career path. Think of it like a garden—the company provides the soil, but you must plant, water, and nurture your growth.

> Myth 2: You cannot switch industries or domains after spending significant time in one.

Piyush: So, if I've been in marketing for ten years, switching to tech is out of the question?

Coach Ram: Not at all! Many people successfully switch industries. It's about leveraging your transferable skills and being willing to learn new things. Industries value fresh perspectives. It's like switching from playing soccer to basketball—the skills of teamwork and strategy still apply.

Myth 3: You need to have graduated from an elite college to reach high levels in an organization.

Piyush: But don't top companies only hire from top schools?

Coach Ram: While elite colleges can open doors, they're not the only path to success. Many successful leaders didn't go to Ivy League schools. What matters more is your performance, skills, and attitude. It's like starting a race—an elite college might give you a head start, but it doesn't guarantee you'll finish first.

Myth 4: A sabbatical derails your career.

Piyush: I've always worried that a career break would ruin my career.

Coach Ram: Taking a sabbatical can enrich your career. It gives you time to recharge, learn new skills, or gain new experiences. When you return, you might have a fresh perspective that makes you more valuable. Think of it as pausing a movie—the story isn't over, you're just taking a break.

Myth 5: High CTC means a bigger and better job.

Piyush: Isn't a high salary a sign of a better job?

Coach Ram: Not necessarily. A high salary is not the sole indicator. The quality of a job is about more than just money—it's about growth opportunities, work-life balance, and personal fulfillment. It's like buying a car—the price tag doesn't always reflect its value to you.

Myth 6: Freelancing or gig work is not a long-term career option.

Piyush: But can you really build a stable career as a freelancer?

Coach Ram: Absolutely. Freelancing offers flexibility and a chance to work on diverse projects. Many people build successful long-term careers this way. It's about managing your workload and finding consistent clients. Think of it as running your own small business—with the right strategy, it can thrive.

Myth 7: Introverts cannot be good leaders.

Piyush: Aren't extroverts natural leaders?

Coach Ram: Introverts can also be excellent leaders. They often bring qualities like active listening, cautious decision-making, humility, and empathy. Leadership isn't about being the loudest in the room; it's about guiding and inspiring others. It's like comparing different musical instruments—each has its unique sound and strength.

Myth 8: Designation and team size are the main indicators of success.

Piyush: Doesn't a big title and large team mean you've made it?

Coach Ram: Again, not a sole indicator. Some roles, which I like to call crucibles (even if they are individual contributors) might offer you a lot of learning opportunities to add value to the organization. These experiences prepare you for a role with a wider span. So, let's not judge a role in isolation.

Piyush: Yes, I see the point now.

Myth 9: Certifications and higher education guarantee new job opportunities or promotions.

Piyush: So, getting more degrees and certificates isn't always the answer?

Coach Ram: They can help, but they're not a guarantee. Your experience, skills, and how you apply your knowledge matter more. Think of certifications as tools in your toolbox—useful, but only if you know how to use them.

Myth 10: Job hopping is bad.

Piyush: But staying in one job for a long time is better for our resume.

Coach Ram: Not necessarily. I would say role-hopping is an advantage. Whether you change organizations or not is secondary. Job hopping can be positive if you gain valuable experience and grow your skills. If a job hopper can't handle the pressure, that's a bad outcome. Employers today often appreciate diverse experiences.

It's like tasting different cuisines—each one adds to your culinary knowledge.

Piyush: Wow, Coach Ram, this changes how I view my career.

Coach Ram: That's the idea, Piyush. Understanding these myths helps you make informed decisions. The corporate world is complex. With the right mindset, you can navigate it successfully. Remember, it's your career—take charge of it!

Piyush: Yes, Coach. What would you suggest as a guiding principle for a professional to navigate these myths and phases?

Coach Ram: I would recommend PIVOT. It's a mindset that turns change from a challenge into an opportunity. PIVOT stands for being Proactive, Informed, Value-driven, Outcome-focused, and Targeted. Take charge of your decisions, stay informed about industry trends, align your choices with your values, focus on outcomes, and set targeted goals.

Piyush: PIVOT. How can we apply it to our profession?

Coach Ram: Let's break it down. Being proactive means taking charge of your decisions. Staying informed involves keeping yourself updated on industry trends. Being value-driven means aligning your choices with your core values. Focusing on outcomes helps you set clear goals. Being targeted ensures that your efforts go toward those goals.

Piyush: Coach Ram, I can see how adopting this mindset can make a difference. But what about the fears that come with career transitions? How does one overcome them?

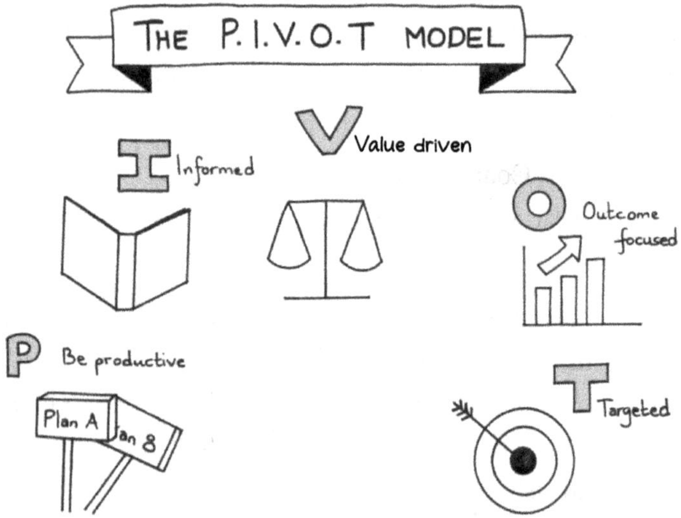

Coach Ram: Fears are natural, Piyush, especially when facing the unknown. Let's address a few common fears. The fear of starting from scratch is rooted in the misconception that previous experiences become irrelevant. Every experience contributes to your skill set and knowledge. It's about repackaging yourself, not starting from zero.

Piyush: That's reassuring. What about the fear of failure?

Coach Ram: The fear of failure is a universal concern. However, let's redefine failure. Instead of seeing it as a dead end, view it as a learning opportunity. Thomas Edison once said, "I have not failed. I've just found 10,000 ways that won't work." Each setback is a step toward success.

Piyush: And what if the new role doesn't match our expectations?

Coach Ram: Managing expectations is crucial. It's about aligning your aspirations with the reality of the new role. Before making a transition, gather information, talk to professionals in that field, and understand the day-to-day responsibilities. All these help in setting realistic expectations.

Piyush: The fear of being overlooked due to age or experience gap is common.

Coach Ram: Age should never be a barrier. Your experience is an asset, not a liability. It's about presenting it in a way that highlights your adaptability and the value you bring. Age brings wisdom and a seasoned perspective—qualities that many organizations value.

Piyush: These insights are invaluable, Coach Ram. They make the whole process seem less intimidating.

Coach Ram: I'm glad to hear that, Piyush. Remember, a career transition is a narrative you create. It can add depth and richness to your professional story. Now, let's discuss the uniqueness of your experience.

Piyush: What do you mean by the uniqueness of my experience?

Coach Ram: Your career journey is as unique as your thumbprint. No one else has followed the exact path, encountered the same challenges, or gained the same insights as you. Recognizing this uniqueness is empowering. Celebrate your diverse skills, perspectives, and strengths that you bring to the table.

Piyush: So, embracing my unique journey becomes a strength rather than a limitation.

Coach Ram: Your experiences, even the challenges, contribute to the richness of your career. Embrace them, and others will see the value you bring.

Self-Coaching Questions

- What achievements or successes from your past roles can you leverage in a new career?
- What are your passions or interests that you haven't explored in your current career?
- What positive affirmations can you give yourself while dealing with the uncertainties of a career change?
- In what ways can you turn potential setbacks or challenges into learning opportunities?

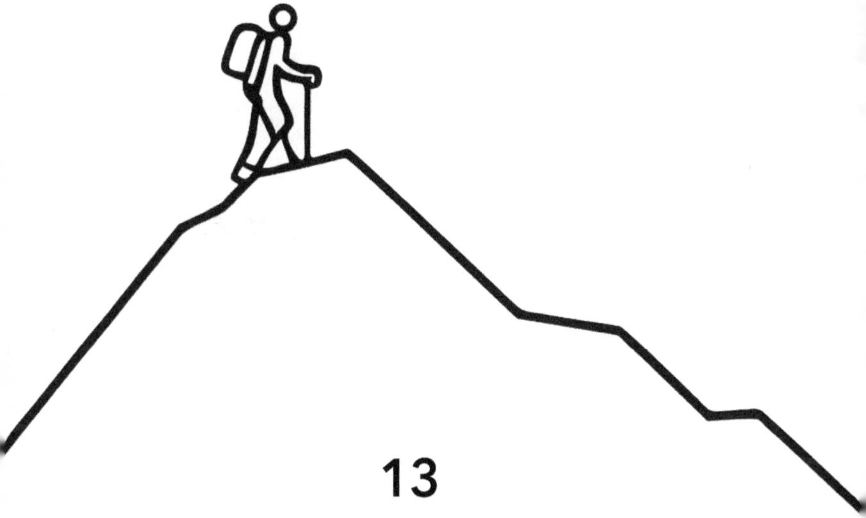

13

Future-Proofing Your Career

Build a career for long-term success

In today's fast-changing professional world, future-proofing your career is a necessity. Even if the present seems favorable, you must ensure your actions and skills align with your future.

Self-Reflective Questionnaire

1. Are you worried about or looking forward to the dynamic industry trends in your career?
2. What are you doing to embrace the technological changes in your professional life?
3. What is your attitude towards continuous learning, and how frequently do you engage in skill development activities?

Future-proofing means accepting new industry trends like generative AI and digital marketing tools to benefit ourselves and our companies. It also involves a commitment to learning and staying ahead of the curve to meet the evolving demands of our careers.

Piyush: Coach Ram, with industries changing so quickly, how can someone ensure their career is resilient to these shifts?

Coach Ram: The PIVOT approach does help, Piyush. The key to staying resilient in the face of change is akin to steering a ship through turbulent waters. It's about having a robust compass and adjusting your sails. Let me illustrate this with a story. There was a graphic designer named Neha who found herself in a rapidly evolving industry. She noticed the increasing demand for virtual and augmented reality. Instead of just accepting the change, she embraced it.

Piyush: What did Neha do to future-proof her career?

Coach Ram: Neha recognized that the design landscape was shifting towards virtual experiences. She didn't wait for her skills to become obsolete; instead, she took the initiative. Neha enrolled in courses that covered virtual and augmented reality, understanding that these emerging technologies would play a significant role in the future of design.

Piyush: So, we anticipate where the industry is heading and prepare for it in advance?

Coach Ram: Precisely, Piyush. With future-proofing, you don't just react to change; you anticipate it. Neha foresaw the future of her industry and decided to stay ahead. She wasn't just following the trends but shaping them.

Piyush: But how can someone like Neha identify which trends to focus on? The business world is so dynamic.

Coach Ram: Identifying trends requires a combination of awareness and foresight. Neha was observant of the shifts in her industry. She paid attention to industry publications, attended conferences, and talked to professionals across different domains. This multifaceted approach helped her discern the patterns likely to shape the future of graphic design.

Piyush: So, staying informed and connected is crucial.

Coach Ram: In today's dynamic environment, staying in the loop is non-negotiable. Networking, attending industry events, and watching market trends allow you to spot opportunities and challenges early on. Start with a giving attitude. When you help others without expecting anything in return, you build genuine relationships.

Piyush: So, it's like planting seeds for the future?

Coach Ram: Exactly! Avoid utilitarian networking, where you're only looking for short-term gains. Instead, build an abundance mindset. Think of networking as a long-term investment. When you help others, you create a network that supports you when you need help. It's like karma but for your career!

Piyush: What about technological changes? They seem to happen rapidly.

Coach Ram: True, Piyush. Technology is a significant driver of change. Neha's decision to enroll in courses related to virtual and augmented reality was a smart move to equip herself with the skills demanded by the evolving technological landscape. It's about being proactive in acquiring the skills that are not just relevant today but will be in demand tomorrow.

Piyush: So, continuous learning is a key aspect of future-proofing?

Coach Ram: Absolutely. The concept of 'lifelong learning,' is not just a catchphrase; it's a career imperative. Neha didn't see learning as a one-time activity; she embraced it as an ongoing journey. Continuous learning ensures that you are not just adapting to change but evolving with it.

Piyush: That makes sense. What about the fear that technology could take away our jobs.

Coach Ram: Technology doesn't take away jobs; it enhances them. Think of it as your best friend who pushes you to level up. The real competition is between those avoiding change and those embracing it. Technology is like a friendly nudge to improve how we work.

Piyush: So, if I'm doing a task the same way for a long time, I should look for better ways?

Coach Ram: Exactly! Ask yourself if there's an efficient way to do your tasks. Technology can help you find those ways. It's like having a toolbox with new gadgets that makes your job easier and more fun. And guess what?

It can even introduce you to more friends, like a social connector!

Piyush: Any tips for someone looking to future-proof their career?

Coach Ram: Certainly, Piyush. Here are a few practical tips:

- Stay Informed: Regularly read industry publications, follow thought leaders on social media, and participate in relevant forums. These help you stay abreast of industry trends.
- Networking: Build a professional network. Attend industry events, connect with colleagues, and engage in conversations. Your network can provide insights and opportunities.
- Embrace Technology: Be open to adopting new technologies. Enroll in courses or training programs to acquire skills that align with technological advancements in your field.
- Anticipate Change: Develop a forward-thinking mindset. Try to anticipate how your industry might evolve and make strategic decisions accordingly.
- Continuous Learning: Learning never stops. Whether it's formal education, online courses, or workshops, invest in your skills regularly.
- Adaptability: Cultivate an adaptable mindset. The ability to pivot when needed and embrace

change will be an asset in future-proofing your career.

Piyush: Those are valuable tips, Coach. It seems like future-proofing is not just about reacting to change but actively shaping one's career journey.

Coach Ram: Also, Piyush, future-proofing your career is incomplete without transferable skills. Skills travel with you. That's how you add value in any field.

Piyush: Can you explain transferable skills?

Coach Ram: Think of them as your toolkit. No matter the job or industry you're in, these skills are valuable. Let's categorize them. First, we have smart skills.

Smart skills include analytical thinking, critical thinking, and creative thinking. Analytical thinking is about drawing specific conclusions from observations and facts. It's the synthesis of information and ideas to solve problems.

Piyush: Like putting pieces of a puzzle together?

Coach Ram: Exactly. Then there's critical thinking. It's about reviewing different points of view, making objective judgments, and investigating possible solutions to a problem. You weigh the pros and cons before deciding.

Piyush: So, we must be thorough and not jump to conclusions.

Coach Ram: Yes. Creative thinking is generating new

ideas, solutions, and designs. It's about thinking outside the box. Next, we'll explore people skills.

Piyush: Sure, I'm all ears.

Coach Ram: People skills are your interpersonal skills, coaching and mentoring abilities, public speaking, and counseling skills. Interpersonal skills help you interact with a wide range of people, including understanding body language and cues.

Piyush: So, the point is to be a good team player and communicator?

Coach Ram: Coaching and mentoring involve giving constructive feedback and helping others build their skills. Public speaking is about making presentations and presenting ideas in an engaging way. Counseling is about responding non-judgmentally and building trust.

Piyush: These skills seem essential for leadership, too.

Coach Ram: They are. Now, let's talk about value-addition skills. These are advanced skills that add value to your profile.

Piyush: What kind of skills are we talking about here?

Coach Ram: Advanced writing skills, for example, where you can select, interpret, and organize key ideas clearly and concisely. Research skills involve finding and collecting relevant information, analyzing data, and summarizing findings.

Piyush: So, being able to write and research well is crucial.

Coach Ram: Absolutely. Then, there are financial skills. The ability to read financial statements, understand and improve the financial health of an organization.

Piyush: Those skills sound like they'd be useful in many jobs.

Coach Ram: They are. Then we have digital skills. Understanding how AI works and integrating it into your strategy at work.

Piyush: Being tech-savvy is important these days. What's next?

Coach Ram: Project-related skills include leadership, persuasion, adaptability, and decision-making. Leadership is about motivating and inspiring others. Negotiation and mediation involve resolving conflicts and making compromises.

Piyush: So, being a good leader is critical for providing vision to the team. Persuasion and influencing are about managing multiple stakeholder expectations and interests, right?

Coach Ram: Yes, and supervision is about delegating responsibility and monitoring progress. Persuasion is communicating in a way that you influence decisions. Adaptability is being flexible and tolerant of change.

Piyush: Decision-making is about weighing options and choosing the best one?

Coach Ram: Exactly. Finally, problem-solving skills are about clarifying a problem, evaluating alternatives, and determining the best outcome. Organizational skills help you organize information and people systematically. Planning skills involve planning projects, events, and programs.

Piyush: So, these skills are not specific to any field. They are required everywhere?

Coach Ram: Yes. Build these skills, and you'll always be valuable, no matter how many times you switch careers.

Piyush: Thanks, Coach. This gives me a lot to think about and work on.

Coach Ram: You're welcome, Piyush. Remember, investing in these skills is like investing in your future. They'll keep you adaptable and valuable in any situation.

Self-Coaching Questions

1. How often do you assess industry trends relevant to your career?
2. What are the strengths of your successor? Can they approach your job differently, if so, how?
3. Do you have a clear vision of where your

industry is heading, and are you acquiring the skills accordingly?

4. What is your mindset towards continuous learning—do you see it as a burden or an opportunity for growth?
5. What strategies can you implement to integrate technological advancements into your current role or professional projects?

In the ever-evolving landscape of our professional journeys, the essence of future-proofing our careers becomes paramount. As we navigate the chapters of our work life, the compass guiding us toward resilience and relevance lies within our ability to adapt to industry trends, embrace technological changes, and commit to lifelong learning.

Remember, future-proofing your career isn't just an idea; it's a mindset. Think of your career like a living thing that grows and thrives when you engage with the changes and demands of the professional world.

So, as you future-proof your career, see each change as a chance to set a new course. Embrace the unknown. Continuous learning, using technology, and staying abreast of industry trends will keep you ahead. Like a ship which adjusts its sails to the wind, let your career adapt to the changing times.

As you reflect upon the ideas in this book, let your excitement for the future guide you. The future isn't far away. Future-proof your career to meet present challenges and grab the opportunities that are just around the corner.

Bon voyage on your journey of future-proofing your career!

14

Hard Truths of Corporations

The shocking reality of the corporate world

It's time to face some hard truths about the corporate world. Truths that are left unspoken but are crucial for long-term success. This chapter aims to provide a candid look at the realities of corporate life, offering practical insights and advice that will help you navigate your career with a clear-eyed understanding of what it takes to thrive in this environment.

Coach Ram: Alright, Piyush, ready to hear the ugly truth about companies?

Piyush: Ready, Coach. Lay it on me.

Coach Ram: These are truths that can make or break a career. They're not always pleasant to hear but they are advantageous. Let's dive into these hard truths, shall we?

- Deliver Bad News Immediately: Rip off the Band-Aid. Get the bad news out there quickly. It's tough, but it's better than letting it fester. Imagine you have a thorn in your foot; better to pull it out immediately than let it be and cause more pain.
- Embrace Difficult Conversations: Don't avoid tough talks. The sooner you have them, the better. Delaying difficult conversations only makes it worse, like ignoring a leaky roof during a storm.

- Avoid Office Gossip: Loose lips sink ships. Seriously, no one can keep a secret forever. Stay out of the rumor mill. Gossip is a bad habit; it might seem harmless, but it can destroy relationships and careers.
- Don't Suffer in Silence: Speak up if something is wrong. Silence doesn't solve problems. If you're unhappy or facing issues, address them head-on. It's like being in a sinking boat—don't wait until you're underwater to shout for help.
- Take Up Challenging Assignments: Don't just stick to what you know. Take on new, challenging tasks. That's how you grow. Think of it as weight training for your career—no pain, no gain.
- Look for Diversity in Your Roles: Mix it up. Different roles give you different perspectives. It's like cross-training for your career, making you more versatile and resilient.
- Invest Time in Your Skill Development: Always be learning. Skills have a shelf life—upskill to stay relevant. If you're not improving, you're falling behind. Think of your skills as plants; they need regular watering and care.
- Operate with the Mindset of Two Levels Above Your Role: Think big. Act like you're already in a higher position. It prepares you for the next step. It's like playing chess—think several moves ahead.
- Network for the Future: Networking is a long-

term game. Start now, and don't expect immediate returns. Building relationships is like planting seeds; they need time to grow.

- Build Your Personal Brand Intentionally: Your personal brand is who you are without the title. Build it on purpose, not by accident. Your brand is your professional reputation—cultivate it like a gardener tending to their prized roses.
- Understand Stakeholders' Needs and Deliver: Everyone is different. Get to know what your stakeholders need and make sure you deliver. Act like a chef—know your diners' tastes and serve accordingly.
- Beyond the To-Do List, Have a To-Think List: Don't just do—think. Reflect on how you can improve and innovate. It's like sharpening your tools before using them—planning makes execution better.
- Time Management Is About Energy Management: It's not just about the clock. Manage your energy levels to stay productive. Think of yourself as a battery—know when and how you need to recharge.
- Straight Talk Is Great, but Use Diplomacy and Tact: Be honest but don't be blunt. A little diplomacy goes a long way. It's like seasoning food—too much salt spoils the dish.
- Job Security Is a Myth: Don't rely too much on

loyalty. Job security is never guaranteed. It's like riding a bicycle—if you stop pedaling, you will fall.

- Be Loyal to the Role and Deliver Superior Performance: Do your best in whatever role you are in. Excellence always stands out. Think of yourself as a craftsman—take pride in your work.
- Have a Compass-Based Five-Year Plan and a Bullseye-Based One-Year Plan: Think long-term with a general direction (compass) and short-term with specific goals (bullseye). It's like navigating a journey—know your destination but focus on each step.
- Office Politics Exist: Fairness is rare. Learn to navigate the politics without losing your integrity. It's like a game of poker—play smart but don't cheat.
- Great Leaders Are Rare: Most people will have manager issues. Learn from both the good and bad examples. Leaders are like rare gems; cherish the good ones and learn from the bad ones.
- Don't Get Jailed by Your Job Description: Go beyond what's expected. Good performance will eventually be rewarded. Think of your job description as a baseline, not a ceiling.
- Be the Biggest Marketer of Your Performance: Don't be shy about your achievements. Make sure people know what you've accomplished. It's like lighting a beacon—make sure your light is seen.

- Manager Will Focus on Your Job; You Should Focus on Your Career: Your manager cares about your current role. You need to think about your future.
- Ask Yourself, "What Will Your Successor Do Differently?": This helps you see what you do from a fresh perspective and improve.
- Have Friends Circle Beyond Former Colleagues: Expand your social circle. Don't just stick to people from work. It's like having a balanced diet—variety is key.
- Don't Burn Bridges with Anyone: It's a small world. You never know when paths might cross again. Think of it as maintaining a good reputation—bad news travels fast.
- Look for Whitespaces in the Organization and Volunteer: Find gaps where you can add value. Volunteer for these opportunities. Just like an entrepreneur, spot opportunities where others don't.
- Know the Business of Your Organization: Understand the core business of your company, no matter what role you are in. You will be respected if you dive into your business.

Piyush: That's a comprehensive list. I have a lot to take in.

Coach Ram: Learn these tenets, live by them, and you'll do just fine. Stay smart, proactive, and adaptable. Keep having conversations with your coach and mentor about your career trek.

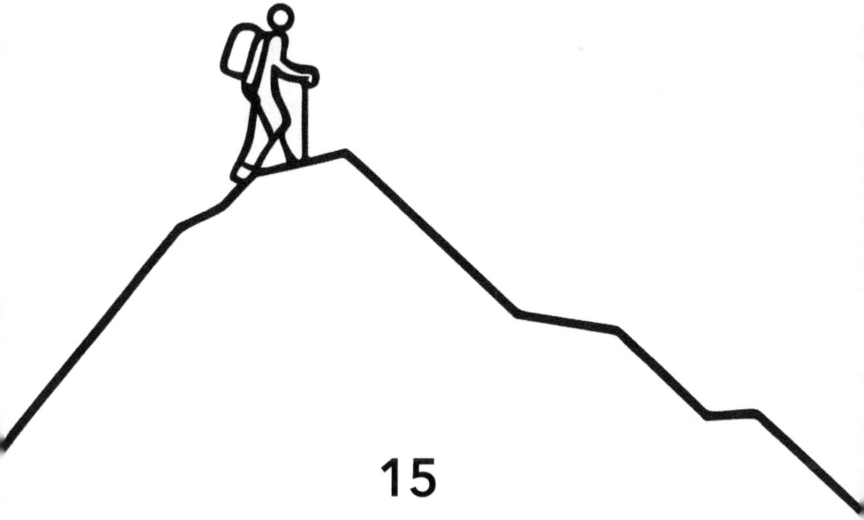

15

Rapid Fire Round with Coach Ram

Coach Ram's quick-fire tips and insights on your career

Q1: New joiners in my company, much younger and paid less, are doing the same role as I am. Should I be worried?

Age and salary should not be your primary concern. Focus on your skills, experience, and unique contributions. If you feel undervalued, discuss your concerns with your superiors and explore opportunities for growth.

Q2: Do you think 10 years of work experience is more valuable than one year of experience repeated 10 times?

One year of experience repeated 10 times lacks learning and growth. Aim for continuous development, take on new challenges, and evolve in your role to maximize your career potential.

Q3: Is the course 'XYZ' good? Should I do it?

The better question is if it will help you progress towards your goals. Evaluate its relevance to your career objectives.

Q4: My career growth has been affected because I don't have a tier-1 MBA. What should I do?

Your growth isn't determined by any one factor, either

positively or negatively. Every career trek is unique. We are a product of our experiences. Find the ocean where you thrive. It's a big world of opportunities out there.

Q5: Should I generalize or specialize? Which has more growth? What suits me?

Assess your strengths and interests. Edgar Schein's *Career Anchors* provide insights. What suits you is more important than growth statistics. Strive for fulfillment over trends.

Q6: Should I have a mentor? How do I choose my mentor?

A mentor provides a telescopic view of your potential. Choose someone trustworthy, challenging, and whose journey aligns with your goals. A close match enhances the mentorship experience.

Q7: How long should I stay in my current role? What is acceptable?

Stay until you haven't hit the legacy phase. Roles evolve in six phases, and two-three years' tenure is best suitable for role change, depending on industry and seniority.

Q8: I want to move to the role or domain 'ABC,' within my company but I am not getting opportunities due to lack of experience.

Build experience and skills through volunteering for extra assignments within or outside your organization.

Q9 What qualities ensure success in the current times?

Explore the OCEAN personality model by Robert McCrae and Paul Costa. Nurture openness, conscientiousness, extraversion, agreeableness, and earning agility for personal and professional growth.

Q10: What tips can help you start well in a new role?

Focus on building relationships, understanding organizational culture, and acknowledging good work done by others. Don't antagonize anyone.

Q11: Coping with frequent changes in managers?

Adapt to different working styles. Align priorities, document progress, and seek alignment with immediate and skip-level managers. Align yourself to your organization's goals and interests more than your manager's goals and interests.

Q12: Big fish in a small pond vs. Small fish in big pond?

Evaluate the advantages of each scenario. Being a big fish in a small pond gives you greater empowerment and responsibility. Being a small fish in a big pond helps gain expertise and skills for enterprise-level challenges. Try both in your career.

Q13: Balancing humility and self-promotion?

Recognize the importance of self-promotion in a competitive environment. Incorporate high-impact storytelling to draw attention to your achievements while maintaining humility. Marketing with substance is key.

Q14: Setting yourself up for success in the current organization?

Consistently add value to customers, peers, and the organization. Foster the growth and independence of team members while making yourself dispensable in your current role. Making yourself dispensable is key to growth.

Q15: How do I deal with competition and attempts at one-upmanship among my peers?

Turn competition into a positive force for collective success. Engage in conversations to understand the aspirations of your peers, fostering collaboration and mutual growth.

Q16: I plan to upskill but struggle to follow through. What's the solution?

Understand the "why" behind the change. Align motivation with goals, create an actionable plan, and build habits. Consider an accountability partner for support and progress monitoring.

Q17: Should I limit myself to the defined role, or should I go beyond?

Job descriptions are starting points, not boundaries. Understand the entire function or business, identify "white spaces," and contribute beyond defined boundaries for role expansion.

Q18: My organization's growth pace doesn't match my aspirations. What should I do?

Align your growth aspirations with the organization's pace or look for another organization that resonates with your aspirations. Seek guidance from mentors, assess your potential, and consider external factors like industry growth in your career plan.

Q19: Should my Individual Development Plan be focused on the organization's needs or personal career needs?

Create your IDP with your manager, ensuring alignment between your goals and organizational priorities. If there is no alignment, then prioritize personal career goals without compromising on performance in your current role.

Q20: I always seek validation from my peers and managers. How do I break out of this loop?

Work on your self-esteem and have clarity on your

career goals. The comparisons and insecurities driven by that will fade away. Remember each of us has unique aspirations and unique career treks.

Q21: Demand opportunities or deserve opportunities. Which approach is better?

Strike a balance between demanding and deserving opportunities. Showcase results, build credibility, and manufacture luck by aligning opportunities with preparedness.

Q22: I need to improve my 'presence' to come across as a capable leader. What should I do?

Improve executive presence by nurturing courage, decisiveness, balance, poise, authenticity, and effective communication. It's the bridge between merit and success.

Q23: My new manager is much younger than me. Any tips for a good working relationship?

Acknowledge your manager's journey and expertise. Have an open conversation about your concerns. Empathize with your manager's perspective. Building trust in the relationship works magic.

Q24: How do we deal with office politics (friendships at work)?

Build clean relationships without gossip. Stay objective

and neutral. Avoid the trap of taking sides. Maintain credibility and trust with all stakeholders.

Q25: What role does emotional intelligence play in career success?

Emotional intelligence is crucial. It enhances interpersonal relationships, communication, and decision-making. Understand and manage your emotions, empathize with others, and navigate social situations effectively for a successful career.

Q26: I feel stuck in my current role. How can I reignite my passion and motivation?

Reconnect with your purpose. Identify tasks you enjoy and align them with your goals. Set new challenges, seek learning opportunities, and consider discussing your career path with a mentor. Rediscover the passion that first drove you.

Q27: My job requires constant collaboration. How can I handle conflicts within the team?

Conflict is natural in collaborative environments. Address issues promptly, encourage open communication, and find common ground. Focus on solutions rather than blame, fostering a positive team dynamic.

Q28: Is networking essential for career growth?

Absolutely. Networking expands your net for

opportunities, provides insights, and builds a professional support system. Attend industry events, connect with colleagues, and engage in professional communities.

Q29: I am considering a career change. How do I make a smooth transition?

Research the desired industry or role, build relevant skills, and network with professionals in the field. Leverage transferable skills from your current role and be open to starting at a comparatively lower level if required. Seek guidance from mentors who have navigated similar transitions.

Q30: How do you maintain a work-life balance in a demanding job?

Set boundaries and prioritize self-care. Delegate tasks when possible, learn to say no, and schedule dedicated time for personal activities. Balancing work and life is essential for long-term success and well-being.

Q31: I'm transitioning to a leadership role. How can I build and lead a successful team?

Understand your team members' strengths and weaknesses. Foster open communication, encourage collaboration, and provide opportunities for professional growth. Lead by example, showing integrity and commitment.

Q32: How do you handle setbacks in your career?

Acknowledge that everyone goes through a phase like this. Don't be bitter or cynical. Analyze the situation, learn from the experience, and adapt your approach. Stay resilient, focus on the lessons learned, and use setbacks as stepping stones to future success.

Q33: I'm considering pursuing further education. How do I decide if it's the right move for my career?

Evaluate the relevance of the education to your career goals. Consider the return on investment, potential networking opportunities, and the impact on your skill set. Ensure the decision aligns with your long-term aspirations.

Q34: How do we stay motivated and avoid burnout in a high-pressure job?

Set realistic goals, establish boundaries, and prioritize self-care. Break down large tasks, celebrate small victories, and maintain a healthy work-life balance. Regularly reassess your priorities to avoid burnout.

Q35: How do I know which profession suits me?

Your free-time activities reveal your likes and what energizes you. Use your experiences as a powerful psychometric tool. Make career choices based on an understanding of yourself. Remember, passion grows on you; it's not just something you discover.

Q36: How do I maximize my potential in the organization?

Reflect on the Zenger-Folkman model to find the sweet spot where your contribution is maximum. Understand and align your strengths with organizational needs for optimal impact and growth.

Q37: I have just taken up a new role. What tips do you have for me to start well?

Don't be desperate to prove yourself; you were hired because they believed you were the right person for the role. Avoid bad-mouthing the status quo or your predecessor's work. Build relationships and blend in, focusing on trust before attempting change. Don't talk too much about how you worked in your previous organization. Find a balance between blending in and bringing your thought leadership to the new role. Challenge the status quo. Don't blindly accept opinions.

Q38: My former boss is calling me to join his team in a new company. Will that be a good move?

Getting an offer from a former boss is a testament to your capabilities. While having a trusting manager is great, assess the opportunity beyond that. Consider the financials, culture, and growth potential of the organization. Review the three-to-five-year growth trajectory of your role before deciding.

Q39: Experts say networking is important. I find it uncomfortable and manipulative. What should I do?

Turn networking into a mission of helping 50 strangers in your industry. Approach it with a zero-return mindset, focusing on giving rather than seeking. As you give, you naturally become a part of the networking process. Networking is vital for success in dynamic times, providing opportunities for learning, perspectives, and future preparation.

Q40: My manager is a control freak and wants to be involved in every detail. What should I do?

Unfortunately, we don't choose our managers. Understand their work style and preferences and meet their needs in the short term to build trust. If stress persists, have an open conversation with your manager. Suffering in silence without dialogue is a common mistake.

Q41: Changing industry mid- career. Is it a good move or not advisable?

Mid-career changes are beneficial. Exposure to multiple industries provides diverse experiences to learn and enrich your professional network. While experience in the same industry can lead to typecasting, breaking out is not impossible.

Q42: There are rough days at work where I feel lonely. How do I cope?

Build an informal 3C network comprising a Confidant, Counsel, and Connections. Share with someone who understands the context, seek advice from a trusted sounding board, and celebrate success with a supportive tribe. Loneliness at work is alleviated by having a best friend within the organization.

Q43: I feel capable of getting the job done, but my managers trust an external consultant more than me. How do I deal with this situation?

Organizations handle some tasks internally, others with the help of external consultants, and at times, a combination of both. When managers decide whom to designate the project to, there are many factors at play, including the skills the job demands. When we are not chosen, it's easy to conclude that we aren't capable. However, we should focus on what the management expects from us instead of all that we are capable of. Second-guessing our boss's thoughts can be frustrating. Having an open conversation is more helpful, even if the news isn't what we want to hear.

Q44: People less capable than me are progressing in their career and getting paid more than me. How do I deal with a lack of parity?

Career growth depends on many factors. When comparing our progress to others, we can't know all the details for an apple-to-apple comparison. No matter how capable we are, there will always be someone who fares better than us. So, parity or fairness may seem like a myth. What we want for ourselves sets our benchmark for parity and that changes based on the people we meet and the information we get from them. For career growth and fulfillment, it's better to focus on internal benchmarks like our purpose, values, culture and compensation rather than just external ones like salary, title, or brand.

Q45: How should I conduct myself during my notice period?

Your behavior during the notice period should stay the same as usual. The trust and goodwill you built during your tenure can get washed away if you behave irresponsibly during your notice period. Irrespective of how you were treated, don't burn your bridges with the organization or your co-workers. Boomerang or rejoining the previous employer is becoming more common. Your relationship with the previous organization can serve as a safety net if the new organization isn't a good fit for you. Your reputation matters more than the job changes you make.

Q46: I regret a career decision I made, and I am not able to get past that. What should I do?

It is hard to find someone who does not have regrets. The question to think on is, "What have I learned from this regret?" We make decisions based on what seemed like the best outcome at that point in time. Dwelling on guilt keeps us stuck. It's better to focus on improving our decision-making skills. Easier said than done, of course. Talk to your coach. We spend too much time reliving our regrets. This keeps us from moving forward. Why turn a flop movie into a hit by playing it so many times in our head? Own your mistakes and make your peace.

Q47: I have had great success working with one manager or organization for many years. But, I am not experiencing the same success with a different manager or organization. What should I do?

While we all know 'change' is the only constant, we resist it. Working with the same manager or organization for an extended period creates familiarity, even if it may not be comfortable for us. Staying in the same environment can limit our professional growth. To eventually lead the company we work for, we need to bring diversity of work environments, cultures, and opinions gathered from people dissimilar to us. We may long to get back to the high points in our career. But reminiscing on past glories cannot prepare us for the challenges of the future.

Q48: I want to grow at a T20 pace. But my organization provides test-match pace growth. What should I do?

Is the industry you are in growing at a fast pace? Is the organization you are in growing at a fast pace? Are you seen as a top talent by your organization? Have you assessed your talents through a professional? Are you resilient and bullish or wishful and dreamy? Several factors need to align for a fast-track career path. Often, you cannot grow faster than your organization or industry. Ask yourself if you are in the right place? We may view ourselves as high-potential super performers but the management could have a different opinion. It behooves us to reflect on the inconsistency. A good career can help you see reality and provide a plan that matches with your aspirations.

Q49: Which type of recognition do you value more: internal or external?

This is a debatable one. I have seen both internal and external recognition forums fail. A leader feels compelled to make everyone happy and awards employees in a round robin. This devalues recognition. I have seen external R&R forums where everyone who nominates themselves gets an award in some category or the other. It's plain to see that the categories were created to keep people happy. This attempt again devalues recognition.

When done right, the recognition forums (both internal and external) help create a culture of excellence that benefits both the individual and the organization and ultimately helps the industry.

Q50: When and how do I have career conversations with my manager?

A conversation with the manager on a promotion, increment, or role change is always a tricky one. The timing of the conversation, your tone or tenor, and approach will decide whether it is perceived as a threatening response or a developmental conversation.

Timing: Are you asking something for yourself now or working towards something in the future? For example, are you negotiating for an increment with a job offer in hand vs. talking about compensation revision commensurate with the role you are in. Conversations ahead of time work better both for the manager and you.

Tone or tenor: Determine if your approach is more of an ultimatum or a way to seek support or partnership to alleviate your concerns. No one likes to feel cornered, nor does your manager. Have a quarterly career conversation with your manager and a half-yearly with your skip-level manager to discuss your development roadmap for the next two years.

Most importantly, go with an open mind and not a demand list. You may end up getting more than what you demand for yourself.

JAICO PUBLISHING HOUSE

Elevate Your Life. Transform Your World.

ESTABLISHED IN 1946, Jaico Publishing House is home to world-transforming authors such as Robin Sharma, Sadhguru, Osho, the Dalai Lama, Deepak Chopra, Eknath Easwaran, Paramhansa Yogananda, Devdutt Pattanaik, Radhakrishnan Pillai, Morgan Housel, Napoleon Hill, John Maxwell, Brian Tracy, and Stephen Hawking.

Our late founder Mr. Jaman Shah first established Jaico as a book distribution company. Sensing that independence was around the corner, he aptly named his company Jaico ('Jai' means victory in Hindi). In order to service the significant demand for affordable books in a developing nation, Mr. Shah initiated Jaico's own publications. Jaico was India's first publisher of paperback books in the English language.

While self-help; religion and philosophy; mind, body and spirit; and business titles form the cornerstone of our non-fiction list, we publish an exciting range of current affairs, history, biography, art and architecture, travel, and popular science books as well. Our renewed focus on popular fiction is evident in our new titles by a host of fresh young talent from India and abroad.

Jaico's translations division publishes select bestselling titles in over 10 regional languages including Gujarati, Hindi, Kannada, Malayalam, Marathi, Tamil, and Telugu. These include titles from renowned national and international authors like Sudha Murthy, Gaur Gopal Das, Swami Mukundananda, Jay Shetty, Simon Sinek, Ankur Warikoo and Jeff Keller.

Visit our Website

Boasting one of India's largest book distribution networks, Jaico has its headquarters in Mumbai, with branches in Ahmedabad, Bangalore, Chennai, Delhi, Hyderabad, and Kolkata. This network ensures that our books reach all parts of the country, both urban and rural.

www.ingramcontent.com/pod-product-compliance
Lightning Source LLC
Chambersburg PA
CBHW071546200326
41519CB00021BB/6632
* 9 7 8 9 3 4 9 3 5 8 8 7 4 *